W9-CZU-354

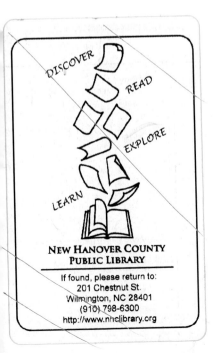

DISCOVER

READ

EXPLORE

LEARN

NEW HANOVER COUNTY
PUBLIC LIBRARY

If found, please return to:
201 Chestnut St.
Wilmington, NC 28401
(910) 798-6300
http://www.nhclibrary.org

Chasing Moonlight

Chasing Moonlight

The True Story of
Field of Dreams'
Doc Graham

BRETT FRIEDLANDER AND
ROBERT REISING

FOREWORD BY DR. BOBBY BROWN

John F. Blair, Publisher
Winston-Salem, North Carolina

JOHN F. BLAIR
PUBLISHER
1406 Plaza Drive
Winston-Salem, North Carolina 27103
www.blairpub.com

Copyright © 2009 by Brett Friedlander and Robert Reising

Manufactured in the United States of America

COVER IMAGE
MOONLIGHT GRAHAM PRACTICING IN HIS GIANTS UNIFORM
Courtesy of the Lynn Williamson Didier Collection

Library of Congress Cataloging-in-Publication Data

Friedlander, Brett.
    Chasing Moonlight : the true story of Field of dreams' Doc Graham / by Brett Friedlander and Robert Reising ; foreword by Dr. Bobby Brown.
        p.   cm.
    Includes index.
    ISBN-13: 978-0-89587-369-9 (alk. paper)
    ISBN-10: 0-89587-369-9 (alk. paper)
    1. Graham, Doc, 1879–1965. 2. Baseball players—United States—Biography. 3. Field of dreams (Motion picture) I. Reising, Robert. II. Title.

GV865.G65F75 2009
796.357092—dc22
[B]
                    2008053960

www.blairpub.com

Design by Debra Long Hampton

To Karen, Erika, and Paul, without whose love and encouragement the dream of this book would never have become a reality

Brett

To my wife, Judy, who has been my strength even when she hasn't always felt so strong

Bob

And to Veda, Ron, and all the other kind, generous citizens of Chisholm, Minnesota, who helped make it possible to bring Doc Graham's story to life

Contents

Foreword

As a physician who also played professional baseball, I can relate to the story of Doc Graham from the movie *Field of Dreams.* He was certainly a memorable figure who inspired a lot of people. But he played ball during the summer when he wasn't in school, and that was a big difference from what I did. We had to play while we were in school. It wasn't a question of just playing during summer vacation. We started when the season opened and played until the season ended, then we caught up in med school. You either had to make up classes when you got back to school or stay longer in order to finish.

The one year I had that was very tough was when I went into my junior year, because I was six weeks behind the class. In the month of September, they all took what is called physical diagnosis. They learned how to take blood pressures, how to listen to the heart, how to examine patients, how to listen to the lungs, how to palpitate the abdomen, and so forth. When I got back, they were already into their clinical work and getting patients to work up and examine. I had to hire tutors to get me through that course while I was also in the regular class. It was a very difficult time for me. I had classes from eight in the morning until nine at night, then I had to do all the rest of the work after that. I finally caught the class at Christmas.

George Medich, an orthopedic surgeon who played 11 major league seasons from 1972 to 1982, had it a little easier because he was a pitcher, and it wasn't as difficult to stay in shape as it was for an everyday player. But he had a lot of the same problems I did. I'm sure Moonlight Graham did, too.

The first two years are mostly the basic sciences. You're taking gross anatomy, microbiology, embryology, biochemistry, pathology, pharmacology—all the courses. They give you the background to start seeing human patients. That comes at the beginning of the third year. The curriculum may be different now. They may have students start seeing patients sooner, but that's the way we did it when I was in med school.

I started in December 1944, during World War II. I was in the navy at the time, and they assigned me to Tulane. That's how I got there. The big advantage I had is that I'd already made it through my first year and was halfway through my second year when I signed with the Yankees in 1946. They knew I could do the work. It wasn't a matter of whether I could do it, because I'd already passed. Still, there was a lot of debate when all this was going on. Nobody knew about Graham when I came along. As far as we knew, playing baseball while going to med school had never been done before. Fortunately, I had some of the faculty go to bat for me. I was a decent student, and since I was already almost halfway through the program, they decided to let me try to do both. The dean, Hiram Watkins Kostmayer, was very supportive. I couldn't have done it without him.

I also got a lot of help from my baseball coach at Stanford my freshman year. His best friend was the president of the

Southern Pacific Railroad, and they had a 500-bed hospital for their 80,000 employees. He told me that if I wanted to intern there for six months a year, then go play ball, I could do it. I did that for two years. Because of my schedule, I never really had spring training. The year I signed, I got over there about the third week in March. In '47, I got there in time because I was able to complete my second year. From '48 on, I would get there somewhere between the first and the 15th of April.

The mental part of it wasn't so bad because once I left med school, got a bat in my hand, and saw that first curve ball, I knew where I was. There was no big adjustment. It's the same when I left baseball for school. I would be back in class in three days. I'd get the homework assignments and forget very quickly that I was a ballplayer. There was no in-between. Physically, it was much tougher. I didn't have any baseball games under my belt. If I could get there 10 days ahead of time, I might get three or four spring games. But if I got there on opening day, I had to start right away from scratch. That's the way it was most of my career.

After my first year, I realized that I couldn't stop playing. So when I got back to school, I would work out every day so that I'd never get out of shape. I did something for at least an hour. I ran, threw a ball, swung a bat. I tried to get kids to throw batting practice for me. The problem was always getting my timing with my hitting, and you have to play games to get that. But it was a small sacrifice. Like Doc Graham, I was fortunate that I didn't have to choose between the two things I loved most—playing baseball and studying medicine—and was able to do both.

Dr. Bobby Brown
Former New York Yankees infielder,
American League president,
and cardiologist

Chasing Moonlight

Introduction
Chasing Moonlight

"What's so special about a half an inning that would make you want to come all the way from Iowa to talk about it 50 years after it happened?"

LATE IN THE AFTERNOON ON JUNE 29, 1905, a kid called Moonlight squinted into a sunlit sky so bright that it hurt his eyes, bolted out of the New York Giants' dugout, and took up his position in right field for the first and only time as a major league baseball player. It was an event of such little consequence that even those who remained that day from the announced crowd of 2,000 at Brooklyn's Washington Park didn't take notice.

And yet a century later, Archibald "Moonlight" Graham has become so well known that a film crew traveled all the way from Tokyo, Japan, to create a documentary on him and a California company trademarked his name for its line of baseball-themed apparel. Moonlight Graham has also become the inspiration for an Ohio-based country folk band

and a charitable foundation that donates thousands of dollars annually to college-bound students. The scholarships, funded solely through the sale of baseball cards bearing his likeness, are as popular as ever nearly 20 years after they were introduced.

No one in the ballpark on that otherwise ordinary afternoon could have imagined that pilgrims would one day journey to Graham's grave site to leave candy, coins, baseballs, and other tokens of gratitude and esteem. Or that the Minnesota Twins would play a tribute game in his honor, marking the 100th anniversary of his flash of major league glory.

So what was it about that half an inning that makes so many people want to talk about it so many years later?

For starters, it wasn't actually half an inning. According to the *New York Evening Telegram* in a two-paragraph account, Graham played "two joyous innings in the right garden while George Browne hustled into his street clothes." Graham even held a bat anxiously in his hands as he waited in the on-deck circle while a teammate made the final out in the Giants' 11–1 victory against the team that would become known as the Dodgers. Shortly thereafter, the 25-year-old journeyman—who spent his off-seasons "moonlighting" as a medical student—was sent back to the minors and presumably into permanent obscurity. His blink of a career was so nondescript that few of his friends and most of the patients he cared for as a successful rural doctor never knew about it.

All he left behind from his crowning moment on the diamond was a single line on page 955 of the *Baseball Encyclopedia*, between the entries for Lee Graham and George Frederick "Peaches" Graham. That and a yellowing photograph of an ambitious young man with oversized ears, a set of pronounced black eyebrows, and the letters *N* and *Y* proudly emblazoned across the chest of his uniform. In fiction, Moonlight would

A.W. "MOONLIGHT" GRAHAM

Height: 5'10.5" Weight: 170
Bats: Left Throws: Right

G	AB	H	2B	3B	HR	R	RBI	BB	SB	SO	AVG
1	0	0	0	0	0	0	0	0	0	0	.000

Following a highly successful minor league career with the Charlotte Hornets of the North Carolina League, Archibald Wright Graham made his major league debut on June 29, 1905, with the New York Giants. It was the same day he retired from professional baseball. With a ten run lead over the Brooklyn Dodgers after eight innings, Giant manager John McGraw made a defensive change, replacing George Browne with "Moonlight" Graham in right field. In less than five —FIVE —minutes, three quick infield outs by the Dodgers ended the game, along with Graham's only chance to face a big league pitcher. While the Giants went on to defeat the Philadelphia Athletics four games to one in the 1905 World Series, Graham left baseball to fulfill his life's work in Chisholm, Minnesota, the year following the Great Chisholm Fire of 1908. "Doc" Graham spent his first six years practicing medicine at Chisholm's Rood Hospital and the next 44(!) years as physician for the Chisholm schools, where he gained national recognition for his thirteen year study of children's blood pressure, as well as the love and respect of the entire Chisholm community.

Moonlight Graham finally did get his time at bat in the 1989 motion picture Field of Dreams. Facing Chicago White Sox pitcher Eddie Cicotte (played by actor Steve Eastin), the young Archie Graham (Frank Whaley) drove in a run by slapping a sacrifice fly to right field.

But earlier in the film when Ray Kinsella (Kevin Costner) commented that the baseball career and lifelong dream of Moonlight Graham (Burt Lancaster) had lasted only five minutes and would be considered a tragedy by many people, Doc Graham replied, "Son, if I'd only got to be a doctor for five minutes, now *that* would have been a tragedy."

A. W. "Moonlight" Graham
N. Y. Giants - Outfield

Baseball card commemorating the 100th anniversary of Graham's one major league game
COURTESY OF
MIKE KALIBABKY,
DOC GRAHAM
SCHOLARSHIP FUND

later say that his fleeting encounter with fame was like coming within an eyelash of his dream, "only to have it brush past you like a stranger in a crowd."

Fate and Graham's long-lost dream finally collided head-on 10 years after his 1965 death, when author W. P. Kinsella stumbled across his record while researching a book on the legendary Shoeless Joe Jackson. During his formative years, through stories told to him by his father, Kinsella had become obsessed with the disgraced Chicago White Sox star. The yarns were only loosely based on fact and tended to glorify Jackson, the best and most popular player of his day. Kinsella grew up believing that his father's hero had been wrongly banned from baseball for his alleged participation in throwing the 1919 World Series. Years later, the aspiring author began weaving his own tall tale about Jackson. After writing a short story in which Jackson returned from the grave to seek redemption and another chance to play the game he loved amid the cornfields of Iowa, he decided to expand the story into what became the award-winning novel *Shoeless Joe.*

That's when Kinsella ran across another old ballplayer in need of a second chance.

The name was the first thing to catch Kinsella's eye. *Moonlight Graham.* It was so distinctive and so poetic that it seemed better than anything he could possibly invent. The fact that the obscure former Giant never got to bat in the majors made him all the more interesting. Kinsella was so intrigued by Graham that he decided to use his name for a secondary character in *Shoeless Joe.* But the more Kinsella thought about the man behind the catchy name, the more he wanted to learn about him.

The questions played in his mind. How was it that Graham played in only one game with the Giants, and why did he not get to bat? More importantly, why would someone born in

North Carolina, the heart of the South, decide to settle in such a cold, remote northern location as Chisholm, Minnesota? "I said to myself, 'There must be a story there,' " Kinsella recalls. "Maybe he'd been exiled or whatever. So I told my wife, 'Let's go up to Chisholm to find out.' " The trip uncovered a life so complex and unusual that Kinsella decided to give Graham a much greater role in the novel.

In fiction, Graham finally got to fulfill his missed destiny by coming back to life with other ghostly players and slapping a sacrifice fly to right field against White Sox pitcher Eddie Cicotte. Though embellished by fiction, Graham's story struck a chord with both baseball fans and hopeless romantics, most of whom were shocked to learn that he was actually based on a living, breathing individual. Suddenly, everyone wanted to know more about the mysterious young ballplayer turned doctor who never got to bat in the major leagues.

One of those new fans, Hollywood director and screenwriter Phil Alden Robinson, decided that Graham deserved a larger audience. In 1989, his adaptation of *Shoeless Joe* was released to the moviegoing public under the title *Field of Dreams,* with Academy Award–winning actor Burt Lancaster as the beloved Doc Graham in what would be his final screen appearance. In the process, Graham endeared himself to viewers in ways no one—not Kinsella, Robinson, or even Graham himself—could ever have imagined. *Field of Dreams* became an immediate cinematic classic. And when it did, the little-known country doctor became an international icon—a man whose longing to bat in the majors became a reality only on a dream-inspired diamond near the town of Dyersville, Iowa. More than a million people have since traveled to the corn-framed movie set in hopes that some of Graham's baseball magic might be channeled into their own lives.

Both Kinsella and Robinson chased Moonlight hard, and

each managed to create an engaging, larger-than-life personality. But neither came close to communicating the character and complexity of the quiet North Carolina native who spent the bulk of his adult life isolated in a small, out-of-the-way town not far from the Canadian border. Kinsella said as much when he admitted that, as a fiction writer, he resorted to inventing facts about Graham's life when he couldn't find them.

Shoeless Joe and *Field of Dreams* were both successes. But Archibald Wright Graham's life merits a much more complete chase and a much more extensive and accurate analysis. A nickname that fired the imagination of a novelist and a script that did no less for a Hollywood legend yielded only a fragment of the narrative that proves not only that truth is stranger than fiction, but that it is no less fascinating than film.

Even now, little is known about Doc Graham, as his friends and acquaintances knew him, other than what Kinsella and Hollywood have told us. That's because he didn't become a public figure until well after his death and because his accomplishments, as profound as they were to the people of Chisholm, were overshadowed by those of his more famous relatives. His father, Alexander, was a superintendent of schools in North Carolina and was so beloved that the *Charlotte Observer* once suggested that "perhaps not a man in [town] was as well-known." His younger brother, Frank Porter Graham, became president of the University of North Carolina, a United States senator, and an early champion of the civil-rights movement. Frank was held in such high regard that he was once offered a chance at the vice presidency by none other than Franklin D. Roosevelt.

Following in the family tradition, Archie was a respected, caring man who dedicated his life to helping others. He became the most popular man in town in both Scranton, Pennsylvania, where he played four seasons of minor league ball, and Chisholm. He simply chose not to call attention to his philanthropy. Instead, he preferred to quietly slip a pair of glasses into the pocket of an indigent youngster or to extend a $10 handshake to a local miner who happened to be down on his luck. He provided health care for generations of children, often going above and beyond the call of duty, and was one of the first to practice what is now called sports medicine. His pioneering research on children's blood pressure is still used at such respected institutions as the Mayo Clinic. With a degree from Johns Hopkins and several internships in New York, Dr. Graham could have practiced anywhere he chose. But he eschewed the lure of the big city to spend 44 years as Chisholm's school doctor.

Such are the contradictions of his life.

He never sought the spotlight but is now a celebrity. He was a generous, down-to-earth man who has become a mythic figure. He loved children and spent the majority of his adult life working among them at a school and yet never had any of his own. A simple small-town doctor seemingly content with his lot in life, he may actually have been haunted by the fact that he came so close to his childhood dream without realizing it. There is much more to the man than one simple line of fine print in the *Baseball Encyclopedia*. Because that one line and the illusion of *Field of Dreams* are all most of us have to go by, the rest of what lurks beneath the "moonlight" is a matter of conjecture.

What might have happened if he had gotten a hit in the major leagues? It's a question characters in the movie openly ponder. If he'd been a success with the Giants, Graham might have stayed in baseball and never become a doctor. While that seems doubtful, given his upbringing and academic foundation, one never knows. In fact, Graham faced several important crossroads that could easily have steered him away from—or at least delayed—his career in medicine and his arrival in Chisholm.

In 1902, Graham's first year as a professional ballplayer, his team was disbanded at midseason because of, among other considerations, a lack of competition. Several members of those Charlotte Hornets, including manager Eddie Ashenback, were picked up by teams in higher leagues and continued to play through the rest of the summer. Graham, who had just earned his undergraduate degree from the University of North Carolina, probably would have done the same had he been among those offered other jobs in baseball. But as a still-unknown rookie, even one with impressive statistics, he was passed over. Instead of playing, he began attending medical school at the University of Maryland in Baltimore.

Eight years later, after getting his license, becoming a doctor, and moving to Minnesota, Graham was offered one final chance to choose the sport he loved over the profession for which he'd been trained when the Boston Red Sox purchased his contract following the 1910 season. This time, he turned down the offer.

When it is suggested to the silver-screen Graham that it might be considered a tragedy by some to leave baseball behind after just five minutes in the majors, the kind old doctor looks his inquisitor squarely in the eye and, with a reassuring grin, gives an answer that has become one of the signature lines of *Field of Dreams.* "Son," he says, "if I'd only gotten to be a doctor for five minutes, now that would have been a tragedy." While the line between fact and fantasy, between legend and legacy, is often blurred regarding the events of Graham's life, at least one thing is irrefutable. The only real tragedy is that the world didn't get to know the good doctor until long after he was gone.

CHAPTER 1

The Beginnings
Books and Balls

"The world knows nothing of its greatest men."
FROM ARCHIE GRAHAM'S ENTRY
IN THE 1905 UNIVERSITY OF
MARYLAND YEARBOOK

IF EVER A MAN WAS DESTINED to achieve greatness, it was Archibald Wright Graham. He arrived into the world in Fayetteville, North Carolina, on November 10, 1879, the second of nine children born to Alexander and Kate Graham. His parents were second-generation Americans descended from "pure" Scottish Highland blood. The family was so well connected that when Archie's great-grandfather Alestair ran afoul of the British Crown for supporting Prince Charles Edward's bid to gain the throne, he was personally transported to America by the legendary naval captain John Paul Jones. The family reached Charleston, South Carolina, in 1780 on the night preceding the surrender of the city to Cornwallis. After a difficult journey, they settled at the home of a relative east of the Cape Fear River, where they would become even more influential and wealthy than they had been back home.

A century later, the area grew into a city known as

Fayetteville, which was primarily a community of workers who toiled for their daily wages at one of the many small textile mills. The Grahams were among the privileged few who had an education and owned their own land. Both Alexander and Kate had already amassed a long list of accomplishments by the time Archie came along.

The family's name was so prominent in the history of early North Carolina that a town named Graham was established in their ancestors' honor. That became a source of great pride to Alexander, who took sport in the connection every time he made the trip by rail from Charlotte to the state capital of Raleigh. As the train prepared to pull into the town's station, a conductor would walk through the car and shout, "Graham!" to which the mischievous school superintendent would reply, "Here I am!" The scene would play out again when the conductor reached the other end of the car. "Graham!" he'd yell. "What do you want with me?" Dr. Graham would ask, a serious look on his face. He would later admit to friends that he pulled the same joke on the same conductor for 20 years, but it never seemed to get old for either.

The family's legacy grew as Alexander and Kate Graham's nine children began to strike out on their own. All of them graduated from college, a rarity in the late 19th century.

By far the most prominent of the children was their youngest son, Frank Porter Graham, who achieved international acclaim during his long and controversial tenure as president of the University of North Carolina. He was also a United States senator and an ambassador to the United Nations whose liberal views on race and public education were years ahead of their time.

David, the eldest, attended Jackson Business College for two years before moving to Chapel Hill, where in addition to earning his bachelor's degree from UNC, he played baseball and served as the personal secretary to the university president, Dr. Francis Preston Venable. He went on to medical school at the University of Maryland before poor eyesight forced him to give up his studies. David eventually went into the electrical business and settled in Philadelphia until enlisting in the Marine Corps prior to World War I. Following in his older brother's footsteps, Archie went to UNC and Maryland and became a doctor,

All but one of the other siblings went into the family business—academics. George was a prominent educator in Atlanta, while sisters Mary and Hattie enjoyed long careers as teachers in the Charlotte school system their father once ran. Mary taught first grade at Myers Park Elementary and was described by former pupil Anne Sarsfield Martin, who went on to become a teacher herself, as a woman who "smiled a lot and laughed a lot." The two youngest Graham girls, Kate and Annie, married university professors and lived in Chapel Hill, where they also dedicated their professional lives to education. Kate said it was a disappointing day when she couldn't make her students laugh.

Another brother, Neill, was a Charlotte lawyer when he died of pneumonia in 1914.

The foundation for all that success was laid by their father, Alexander. He was the first member of the clan to attend UNC, where he was captain of the baseball team and earned a degree before enlisting in the Confederate army late in the Civil War. He fought with the Third Regiment of North Carolina troops in the Battle of Bentonville and was captured by Union soldiers. Upon his release at the end of the war, Alexander Graham moved to New York and earned his law degree from Columbia University. He then returned home to Fayetteville to set up his own practice.

His inspiration to academia was an 1878 trial in which 12

young boys were called to the stand as witnesses. After the verdict, the boys were asked to sign their names for the record. The six black boys did. The six white boys did not know how to write. Disturbed by the incident, Graham began collecting subscriptions ranging from five cents to $250 to help finance a public school system. He ended up raising about $3,500, enough to pay for teachers and a modest building. The following year, he was drafted as Fayetteville's first superintendent of schools, beginning a career that would result in at least two schools being named in his honor and a legacy as "the father of the graded school in North Carolina."

Archie's mother was also a scholar. In 1857, Kathryn Sloan Bryan was the first student to enroll at Peace Institute, a new women's college in Raleigh. A small, dainty woman barely five feet tall with brown hair and brown eyes, she had a cheerful disposition that endeared her to the people of Fayetteville. It was an outlook on life that her second son would inherit and that would help him to become just as beloved to the people of his adult home in Minnesota.

But as much as young Archie adored his mother and picked up some of her most endearing qualities, it was his younger brother Frank who favored her more both in stature and disposition. Frank, who went on to become one of the most charismatic, popular, and controversial figures of his era, was small and reserved. Archie, on the other hand, was athletic and outgoing like his father. In fact, he would grow up to become the spitting image of Alexander Graham.

Like his father, a commanding man with a square jaw, bald head, and features that looked as though they had been chiseled from a block of North Carolina granite, Archie liked to get up early, before either the sun or anyone else in the house made their first appearance of the day. He would read the morning newspaper, bundle himself against the cold, and take long, introspective walks through town on his way to work.

As was the case with his father, finances weren't Archie's strong suit. While Alexander made a good enough living as a school superintendent, he barely had enough money to raise his nine children, pay a house staff, and afford luxuries such as a telephone and electricity. Things got so tight that when it came time to send Frank, the seventh of nine children, to college, the Grahams had to take out a loan for his $265.25 annual tuition at UNC. What little extra money Alexander had in his pockets usually ended up in the hands of children and those less fortunate than the Grahams. Archie grew up to be just as benevolent, showering generations of children in Chisholm, Minnesota, with coins and candy and never bothering to cash the rent checks of his tenants who were down on their luck. Those who knew him described him as real-estate rich and rent poor, though not entirely because of his generosity.

By his own admission, Archie was forgetful at best and absent-minded at worst. His father was just as notorious for his spotty memory, to the point that whenever he came across one of his students walking down the street, he'd stop him and ask, "Hey, boy, what's your name?" On one occasion, he disciplined a group of misbehaving boys by locking them in a toolshed, then forgot about them. When the boys didn't return home after school, their parents started to worry. By dark, they organized a frantic search to find them. Eventually, some of their schoolmates told the nervous parents what had happened, and Superintendent Graham was summoned to unlock the door and let the boys out.

Because there wasn't much to do in Fayetteville at that time other than going to work or school and attending church on Sunday, sports became a favorite pastime for its 17,000 residents, about half of whom were freed slaves. The Graham

Alexander Graham was an athletic man whose features looked as though they were chiseled from North Carolina granite. Like his son, Archie, he was a man of many quirks.
COURTESY OF THE *FAYETTEVILLE OBSERVER*

family was especially active athletically. Not only had Alexander played on the varsity baseball team in college, he was passionate in the belief that nothing contributed to a sound mind more than a healthy body. He made sure that he and his children took part in some kind of exercise each day. Usually, that meant playing ball, but calisthenics were also part of the family's physical fitness regimen.

The Grahams did calisthenics outdoors, though it didn't start out that way. They made the change after an incident involving an old chair that Alexander used to hold tightly in his hands while he stretched his arms in each direction. One day, he lost his grip on the chair, sending it flying into the air. It crashed into Kate Graham's favorite chandelier, making a loud noise and sending shards of crystal in every direction.

When they weren't participating in formal exercises, the Graham children loved to run. While David was by far the best natural athlete, Archie was the fastest of the bunch, regularly beating the others in footraces through the fields behind their house. He also purportedly earned a little extra spending money by challenging and outsprinting his friends.

Baseball, however, was the family's sport of choice, which was fine with an old ballplayer like Alexander Graham. In the spring of 1867, Fayetteville became one of the first towns in North Carolina to form its own team. It was an undertaking the local newspaper endorsed as "beneficial" to the community, especially after "the Lafayette team" beat a squad from Wilmington a year later.

Most baseball was played in Bevels' Pasture, which was exactly what it sounds like—a large, open field where the local boys would gather and toss the ball around once they shooed all the cows out of the way. More organized games among the adults were played at "the Fairgrounds," a ballpark with wooden grandstands that would go on to become a historic landmark when a young man named Jim Thorpe played professional ball there for the Fayetteville Highlanders during the summer of 1910. When it was discovered years later that he'd been paid a few dollars a week for his services on the diamond, Thorpe was stripped of his amateur status and forced to return the gold medals he had won at the 1912 Summer Olympics in Stockholm, Sweden.

Thorpe's most memorable accomplishment at the old Fairgrounds was the home run he hit in 1909 while playing for a visiting team. Witnesses swore it was the longest they'd ever seen. Five years later, a big-boned teenager named George Herman Ruth hit one even farther while playing in a spring training game for the Baltimore Orioles. Newspaper accounts of the prodigious blow marveled over the first professional home run launched by scout Jack Dunn's prized "Babe." Ruth went on to smack 714 of them in the major leagues for the Red Sox, Yankees, and Braves.

Because of his youth, Archie Graham probably never played any games at the old Fairgrounds. Instead, he got most of his early playing experience closer to home. The Grahams lived in a large house located at the top of Harrington Hill near the Tokay Winery. Today, a historic marker honoring Archie's younger brother Frank is located about 50 yards west of the property, which was also known as "Fuller's Place" and later as "the James A. King Place." Although it was located only about five miles from the Victorian houses and tree-shaded streets off Market Square in the center of town, the Graham estate was considered at the time to be far out in the country.

Archie learned to catch and throw in the fields of the old winery from his father and older brother, David, with whom he formed an enduring bond. The two were inseparable as they were growing up. Not only did they play together, they also frequently read and studied together. Archie's fascination with the sciences and medicine—which was different from the rest of the family's obsession with history and education—was a direct result of David's influence. Their relationship was so close that when David joined the Marine Corps nine years before World War I, he listed Archie, rather than his parents, as his next of kin.

While young Archie looked up to David, his own emerging athletic prowess made him something of a heroic figure in his own right to his younger brothers and sisters. Frank in particular dreamed of following in Archie's footsteps as a ballplayer. Mimicking Archie's example, he refrained from smoking and drinking, including cola and coffee, to stay in peak playing condition. But since he was much smaller and frail because of a series of childhood illnesses, Frank wasn't nearly as good as his older brother. That didn't dampen his enthusiasm for the game. He was always the organizer of the neighborhood sandlot games. And like the rest of the Graham children, he loved playing almost from the moment he learned to grip a bat.

It's a passion that never waned, even when he reached high school and began to realize he would never achieve the same kind of success on the diamond enjoyed by Archie. Frank continued to play baseball, defying his physical deficiencies to earn a spot on the varsity baseball team at UNC, just as his father and older brothers had. He also went on to organize and coach his own team once he graduated and became a teacher. But while Archie continued to place a high priority on his athletic endeavors, Frank began to steer his interest more toward academics and the ideal of amateurism.

Years later, as the first president of the consolidated UNC system, he became a central figure in a debate over commercialism and its place in college athletics. Inspired by a 1929

Carnegie Foundation report entitled *American College Athletics,* Frank drafted a radical reform plan that would, among other things, eliminate all athletic scholarships. Though well intentioned and sound in its ideals, "the Graham Plan" went over about as well as an inning-ending double play with the tying run on third. It was vilified by prominent businessmen and athletic boosters, who argued that athletics were an important part of the educational mission of the university and should not be tinkered with. The objections were so strenuous that Frank eventually backed off his crusade, if not his ideals. That became a pattern in his career.

In 1936, he was sitting in his office talking to prominent New York surgeon and UNC alumnus Dr. Miguel Elias when he received a call from the White House. It was President Franklin D. Roosevelt with a stunning request. "I would like to ask you to be my running mate—to run as vice president on my ticket," the United States president told the university president in a conversation documented in the book *Hark the Sound of Tar Heel Voices* by Daniel W. Barefoot. Graham was nearly floored by the invitation. Though flattered, he respectfully turned Roosevelt down. His rationale for the decision was that he was a teacher, not a politician.

That changed in 1949 when he was appointed by Governor Kerr Scott to fill the vacancy in the United States Senate created by the death of J. Melville Broughton. A year later, Moonlight Graham's kid brother found himself in a heated campaign to keep the seat. He easily won the three-man primary in May. But because he failed to win a majority of the votes, he was forced to participate in a runoff for the Democratic nomination. That's when things got ugly. A progressive in the area of civil rights, as all the Grahams were, Frank was portrayed by the opposition as a communist and, worse, a liberal "nigger lover." Leading the angry call was a young columnist for

Frank Porter Graham idolized his big brother and went on to success in his own right as an educator, a United States senator, and an ambassador to the United Nations.
COURTESY OF THE *FAYETTEVILLE OBSERVER*

the *Raleigh Times* named Jesse Helms. Stirring fear with anti-Graham campaign slogans such as "Wake Up, White People," Helms catapulted to prominence and launched a successful career that led to five terms of his own in the Senate. Graham never had a chance under such an onslaught. His opponent, Willis Smith, won 67 percent of the vote and went on to easily defeat Republican E. L. Gavin in November.

The campaign was so bitter and the defeat so disappointing that Frank never sought public office again. Like his brother's major league baseball career, his time in the Senate lasted only long enough to say he was there and no more. At least both had other options on which to fall back. That's because in the Graham household, baseball and politics weren't obsessions but rather pastimes. Archie and his siblings spent considerable time in school and church. The Grahams stressed religion heavily and attended services every Sunday morning. The family's rigid Presbyterianism would years later inspire a distant cousin named Billy Graham. But education was even more important, especially for Archie, whose interest in the abstract teachings of science eventually led him to drift from the church and its teachings.

His fascination with scholarship began around the age of six or seven when he started attending the "graded school" his father helped establish and lead. The school, which had an enrollment of 400 students, was located at the Seminary Building on Hay Street. By that time, the Fayetteville Graded School was well known throughout North Carolina as a model for others to follow. Alexander frequently traveled around the state helping residents in places such as Greensboro and Charlotte set up their own school systems. In 1888, he was hired by the city of Charlotte to become its first school superintendent. At the age of nine, Archie helped his family pack their belongings and leave their country house by the winery to move to a more urban setting.

Charlotte in the late 1880s wasn't the major banking center it is today. The city actually had a slightly smaller population than Fayetteville, but it was still much more modern and vibrant. Its location on the railroad line between Washington, D.C., and Atlanta made it a hub for industry and transportation. Charlotte had five cotton mills, and its streets were crowded with pedestrian traffic and streetcars. Shortly after the Grahams arrived, the horse-drawn coaches were replaced by electric ones, open in the summer and covered in the cold of winter.

As exciting and modern a place as Charlotte was, the Graham clan still found plenty of room to move about. Their two-story brick home at 808 Mount Vernon Avenue had a large yard that became a gathering spot for the neighborhood children. Archie's mother, Kate, would regularly invite them all into the house to listen to a book or to help themselves to her "biscuit drawer," as she called it, where they could always find fresh bread, cookies, and other treats. The children had a swing on the porch, plenty of tall trees to climb, and a large, open field just right for playing hide-and-seek and, of course, baseball. All the local children—black and white, boys and girls—would choose up sides and play until twilight. The practice continued long after Archie was old enough to leave home to attend college.

Growing up in the Graham house was an idyllic existence in which everyone ate, read, and played together as a family. Chores were distributed evenly among the brood. Archie had to take his turn fetching wood for the fireplace and water for the kitchen. Around the dinner table, his father would often steer the discussion toward history, his favorite subject. But as fascinated as he was with the events of the past, Alexander Graham would rarely, if ever, mention his own experiences in the Confederate army. It was the same unspoken philosophy his son would adopt years later toward his major league baseball experience with the New York Giants. After dinner each night, everyone in the household would retire to the living room, where family members would select reading material from the two amply stocked bookshelves that lined the walls.

For the most part, the family got along well. Alexander and Kate rarely argued, and when they did, it was never within earshot of the children. When Archie and his siblings had their periodic spats, order was maintained with a firm, though quiet, hand. And when the children needed someone in whom to confide, they often bypassed their authoritative parents and talked to Anne, the family's Negro cook and housekeeper.

After graduating from high school at Davidson Academy in 1897, Archie continued the Graham tradition by moving to Chapel Hill and enrolling at UNC. There, his warm smile, engaging personality, and well-respected surname helped make him one of the most popular and influential men on campus. He was selected as the sophomore class poet and was a member of the Dialectic Society, the Young Men's Christian Association, the Historical Society, and the Shakespeare Club. He lived in the Old West dormitory, just as his father and brother had before him. His room was a place to which other students gravitated.

Chapel Hill around the turn of the 20th century was much smaller and isolated than it is today. That was by design. When the university's charter was adopted in 1789, it stipulated that the school not be located within five miles of a town in which court was held. The location eventually chosen was a grove at the intersection of two frontier highways near the center of the state. At the time of Archie Graham's enrollment, UNC consisted of about a dozen buildings, all with electric lighting, and a faculty of 67. Although the university was equipped with 11 scientific laboratories, it did not yet have a fully accredited hospital. Because it lacked the facilities for proper clinical instruction, its medical school was limited to just a two-year program. That's why both Archie and his older brother, David, transferred to the University of Maryland—which was located in the urban center of Baltimore and had its own teaching hospital—to finish their medical studies.

Archie played class football during his first two years at UNC and was on the "scrub" squad as a senior. While he would later admit that football was his first love, he was far more accomplished as a baseball player. His baseball career at UNC progressed rapidly. He started on the "scrub" squad, a ragtag unit of extra players who languished at the bottom of the roster and saw action only in games decided by large margins or in preliminaries against the other teams' rejects. He was promoted to the varsity as a sophomore in 1899 and earned the position of starting center fielder as a junior and senior. After graduating with a bachelor's degree in 1901 at the age of 21, Graham returned the following fall as a first-year medical student and played another season in center field for the Tar Heels.

Though individual statistics were not recorded, Graham was undoubtedly one of the best players on his team. His college profile listed him at five-foot-nine, 162 pounds, which was small for a ballplayer even by the standards of the day. But he made up for his lack of size with speed and a deft touch with the bat that allowed him to lay down bunts and slap the ball to the opposite field. He also had a knack for running down and grabbing even the most uncatchable drives into the gap. In his first season with the varsity, the Tar Heels finished 8–1–1. The '01 team went 11–3–2, including a 31–3 drubbing of North Carolina A&T and a 40–0 shellacking of Georgia in

Team photo of the 1901 University of North Carolina baseball squad that went 11–3–2, including a 40–0 shellacking of Georgia. Graham is first on the right on the second row from the top. COURTESY OF UNC LIBRARIES

the season finale. Following the season, Graham played professionally for the first time, though very briefly, for Tarboro of the Virginia–North Carolina League.

The next summer, after Graham played one last season at UNC, his college coach, Eddie Ashenback, convinced the star outfielder to sign a contract and play for him with the Charlotte Hornets of the newly formed North Carolina League. Thus began a practice of moonlighting that would continue for the next eight years. Graham played professional baseball every summer between 1902 and 1908. For at least part of that time, he continued to play collegiately at Maryland while attending medical school.

"They didn't care in those days," Graham said in a 1963 interview with the *Charlotte News*. "Why, to show you how lax the rules were . . . I played halfback for Maryland in the fall and played professional baseball in the summer. Today you can't even accept a free Life Saver while you're playing college athletics."

In 1904 and 1905, Archie Graham didn't enjoy just one free Life Saver. He took the entire roll. In addition to playing football at Maryland, he spent two more seasons on the varsity baseball team—giving him at least five years of college eligibility in total. Even with all that time spent on the playing fields, he still found a way to serve as his class secretary, to be selected as "Demonstrator of Anatomy," and to earn his medical degree.

He was 25 years old now and about to realize his dream of becoming a doctor. At some point soon, he knew he would have to stop performing his annual juggling act, put away his bat and glove, and start getting serious about his chosen career. But with nearly as many offers from major league teams as from major medical centers seeking his services as an intern, he knew that time still hadn't come.

CHAPTER 2

Moonlighting
The Minor League Years

———

"Nicknames are funny. They just land on you like waking up one morning with a tattoo. You don't know how you got it, but you know it's going to be with you forever."

MOONLIGHT GRAHAM IN THE
NOVEL *SHOELESS JOE*

AS NICKNAMES GO, Archie Graham got tagged with a good one—so good that it eventually made him immortal long after he left this mortal world. But for the life of him, he couldn't remember how or when he got tagged with it. Like a mysterious tattoo, it just showed up one morning early in his minor league career.

In *Shoeless Joe*, W. P. Kinsella offers up a detailed—though fictional—explanation in which the young ballplayer has a hard time getting to sleep one night because his roommate, a catcher named Ernie Squim, makes too much noise on the brass bed next to him. Lying there in the darkness and humidity, an uncomfortable Graham describes himself as feeling like "one of those corpses we kept floating in the big glass vats up at [Johns] Hopkins, where I was studying."

Unable to take it anymore, Graham hops out of bed, reaches into the closet, and grabs the first clothes he gets his hands on, which turn out to be his baseball uniform. He dresses and goes outside for a walk under the full moon. It isn't long before he hears his roommate's voice bellowing out the open window at him. "Graham," Squim yells down from the hotel room. "What the heck are you doing standing out there in the moonlight? . . . And you got your uniform on. What are you doing, playing ball out there in the moonlight?" By that time, all the other players on the team have awakened and begin hooting at Graham from their windows. From that moment on, he became known as Moonlight Graham.

Though Kinsella's account makes for an entertaining story, there is absolutely no evidence to support that it ever happened. The truth is likely much less romantic.

One possible explanation was published in the *Brooklyn Eagle* newspaper on March 22, 1905, three months before Graham's two-inning brush with the majors. The item reported that "Archibald Graham of the Baltimore Medical College" would join the New York Giants as soon as he got his degree. The story went on to say that the outfielder was "nicknamed Moonlight by his fellow players on account of his speed."

Graham was in fact a very fast runner. According to early accounts of his minor league career, he could run down fly balls in center field better than anyone. And in each of his last three seasons of organized ball—all with Scranton of the New York State League—he stole 30 or more bases. But since moonlight has never been equated with speed like, say, lightning is, the more likely scenario is that Graham got his nickname simply because he spent his summers moonlighting as a baseball player while he pursued his calling as a doctor.

Such endeavors aren't so uncommon these days, when a large percentage of players attend college and work toward careers outside baseball while they play. But back in the dead-ball era, when professional athletes were usually lower-class street urchins—such as John McGraw—or boys from the Midwest trying to escape the farm, Graham's double duty was highly unusual. While most young gentleman of higher upbringing were encouraged to play football or baseball with the other college boys, few ever seriously considered continuing their careers past graduation. For one thing, professional sports at that time were largely unorganized and ruled by dictatorial owners who paid and treated players as though they were indentured servants. A young man with a college degree could make a much better living as a doctor, lawyer, or champion of commerce. He could maintain a connection to sports by going to the park on sunny afternoons and watching the rough-and-tumble sons of immigrants and uneducated farm boys play ball.

Graham was an exception, though it's doubtful he began playing minor league ball with any realistic aspiration of eventually making it to the majors. His professional experience started out as nothing more than a favor to Eddie Ashenback, his old coach at the University of North Carolina, who also moonlighted by managing the Charlotte Hornets of the North Carolina League in the summer.

Actually, the ambitious outfielder got his first taste of professional ball in 1901, when he played in one game, going 0 for 3, with Tarboro of the Virginia–North Carolina League. The following summer, having just finished his first year of medical school at UNC, he decided it might be fun to help out "Ol' Eddie" and play a little ball. If he could make a few bucks and stay at home with his parents in Charlotte, so much the better.

Young Archie, still a year or two away from picking up his famous nickname, joined the Hornets on June 4, some 25 games into the season. By that time, the Charlotte nine was already tearing up the league. Its 8–3 victory over New Bern the day before Graham's arrival was its 19th straight. Yet despite a league-best 23–3 record, Ashenback decided to change his lineup and insert his newest player right away. Graham made an immediate impression by going 2 for 4 with a double and making plays on all six balls hit to him in left field, leading the Hornets to their 20th consecutive victory, 8–1 against New Bern.

The streak would ultimately grow to 25 games, a "world's record" at the time, celebrated 30 years later by a front-page story in the local newspaper. The most memorable of those games, at least from Graham's perspective, was win number 23, which came on June 8 against Durham.

Though his first few performances didn't suggest it, the full-time med student considered himself a part-time ballplayer. And even at that, he wasn't sure he belonged with the pros. That uncertainty came out in the first inning, when the left-handed hitter, batting cleanup, approached the plate to face Durham's ace, a hard-throwing veteran southpaw named Morris. As if Graham weren't already nervous enough about facing the toughest pitcher he'd ever seen, his trepidation got worse when he was greeted by a large ovation from the crowd of about 500 paying customers who jammed the wooden grandstand at Charlotte's Latta Park.

The newspaper account of the day described Graham "grinning sheepishly" toward his fans and not "looking all that cheerful" as he stepped into the batter's box. In fact, as the *Charlotte Observer* reported, it was an open secret that while he was still on the on-deck circle, Graham begged Ashenback to put someone else in his place.

"I simply can't hit that fellow Morris," the *Observer* quoted Graham as saying to his skipper.

"Just relax and get out there," Ashenback replied quickly and decisively. "You can knock the spots off anything Morris could offer." With that, he pushed the 22-year-old rookie toward home plate like a sheep to slaughter.

Morris certainly thought that was the case. The old pro, who had a habit of staring down opposing batters with a sly smile, grinned ear to ear as he watched the frightened Graham get set, thinking he would be an easy out. Though he started the at-bat "trembling like the star performer at his own wedding," the youngster calmed down as he worked himself deep into the count. By the time Morris delivered a 3–2 fastball through the heart of the plate, Graham had forgotten all about his nerves and let his instincts take over.

"Suddenly he unlimbered, there was a resounding crack and the grandstand showed renewed signs of lunacy," was how the *Observer* described it. "Graham was down like a bird for first while Durham's left fielder, after a hard run, picked up the spheroid as it was rolling into the racetrack. Armstrong scored [from first] in a walk and Graham would have made a home run, but for the fact that in his excitement, he ran over himself between first and second bases and had to catch a new grip on his speed."

Still, he made it all the way to third for a stand-up triple. Graham scored one batter later when Ashenback, who doubled as the Hornets' right fielder, drove him home with a sacrifice fly.

Later, with the score tied at 4 in the bottom of the 10th, Graham was involved in another eventful play when Durham's first baseman, a player named Rockford, faked a throw to third and caught Graham napping off first for an out. The gaffe didn't hurt his team, though, when moments later Morris uncorked a wild pitch to allow Charlotte's Buck Weaver to score the winning run.

That 10th-inning mistake aside, the game was a significant one in Graham's budding baseball career. For the first time, he realized that he was good enough to hold his own with serious professional players and that, possibly, his medical studies notwithstanding, he had a future in the game.

Of course, it was easy to get excited about baseball in Charlotte in the summer of 1902. It was a time of great progress in what was rapidly growing into a major metropolitan area. With the Hornets in the midst of their record success, everyone seemed to get caught up in the moment. "We used to march around the flag pole before the game during our win streak and it used to burn the other ballclubs," Graham told a reporter in 1963 when he returned to Charlotte for a celebration honoring the 1902 club.

Games at Latta Park became community events, drawing crowds of up to 2,500 on Saturdays. Fans paid 25 cents a head to attend. Most of those who came to the games were white adult men dressed in suits and ties, though ladies and children were also welcome at the discounted admission of 15 cents. The brainchild of developer Edward Dilworth Latta, the magnificent (for that era) ballpark was the centerpiece of the new suburb he was building just east of town. The stadium—which featured a covered grandstand and wooden bleachers along the right-field line sporting a large advertisement for Coca-Cola—was so nice that the Philadelphia Phillies had held their spring training camp there in 1899. Two years later, the Brooklyn Dodgers followed suit.

It was the local boys, however, who sparked fans' passions. For nearly a month in 1902, it seemed as though they would never lose again. Needless to say, the Hornets' winning streak didn't play as well elsewhere around the league as it did in Charlotte. By mid-June, rumors began to spread that Ashenback was violating league rules by paying his players too much. When the accusations, put forward mainly by the Durham club, finally became public, the Charlotte manager reacted with righteous indignation. Even though the Hornets probably were breaking the rules, he offered to bring all his players before league president Perrin Busbee so that they could sign a notarized affidavit disclosing the amount they were being paid and prove their innocence.

"I am getting tired of the way Charlotte is being treated," Ashenback said. "Our attendance here at home is nearly double that in other cities. . . . Charlotte virtually supports the whole league." He then threatened to take his team elsewhere if the accusations didn't stop, hinting that he would pull out of the North Carolina League by starting one of his own, which would encompass cities in both North and South Carolina.

If the controversy was meant as a distraction to the talented Hornets, it didn't work. They won twice more to run their winning streak to 25 before Durham spoiled the party with a 13–8 triumph on June 11. As if they were satisfied at finally beating their most bitter rival, the third-place Bulls withdrew their protest over Charlotte's salaries the next day at a meeting of the league's executive committee. Ashenback, who represented his team in Raleigh, left the meeting feeling vindicated. He then boarded a train for New Bern, where the Hornets began a new winning streak by winning 5–2 behind a pair of doubles by Graham. A little more than two weeks later, Charlotte finished at 39–8 for the season's first half—12 games ahead of second-place Raleigh—by beating Greensboro 5–1.

Through it all, Graham continued to play well. On June 23, the slender outfielder singled four times in five trips to the plate, stole two bases, and made a spectacular running catch.

"In field work and in base running," the *Charlotte Observer* reported the next day, "Graham showed at his best and was a decided favorite." At the midway break in the season, he was hitting a hefty .321, third best on the team.

But the good times didn't last. After the Hornets lost 7–1 to Raleigh in the opening game of the second half, it came to light that Ashenback was being courted to play for and manage the Cincinnati Reds. With their leader looking to get out and predictions that the North Carolina League was losing money, Graham and his teammates suddenly started to worry that their dream season might not reach its expected conclusion.

Such circumstances were not unusual in the early years of professional baseball. Teams and even entire leagues came and went as rapidly as the latest fads in clothing or music, often abruptly disappearing in the middle of a season. Because of that uncertainty, the hired help tended to be equally unsettled. Unencumbered by formal agreements that bound them to teams, players routinely broke their contracts. If they sensed that their owner might be having difficulty making payroll or that their league might be in trouble, they didn't think twice about jumping ship the moment anybody presented them with a better offer to play somewhere else.

The Hornets' fears began to take hold on July 5 when the Wilmington team disbanded and its players were sold off to teams in other leagues. By July 13, the league was officially on its last legs. On that day, Graham and the other Hornets were handed telegrams informing them that their team had been taken over by the league. They were instructed to report to Commissioner Busbee's office in Raleigh the following day for allotment to other teams. They were also warned that any player who failed to comply would be blacklisted. They need not have worried. Before they could ever board a train and leave Charlotte, New Bern announced that it was pulling out of the league.

Instead of going to Raleigh to meet with the commissioner, the Hornets started dispersing on their own. Ashenback was the first to go, taking two of his players—third baseman Art Brouthers and shortstop Champ Osteen—with him. Before leaving, he fired off a parting shot in a telegram to Busbee. "Farewell, president," he wrote. "I am leaving for Cincinnati. Will send Osteen and Brouthers to you when chloroformed or drunk." Within the next few days, pitcher Eddie Persons left for Shreveport, Louisiana, while center fielder Weaver and another pitcher, Fred Applegate, headed to Newark, New Jersey. When the exodus was joined by players from other teams, the North Carolina League was officially dead.

Despite batting .297 (33 for 111) with 17 stolen bases, Graham wasn't among those who went on to play elsewhere. It was probably for the best. Playing a summer of professional baseball and proving he belonged was fun. But with school getting ready to start again in the fall and a career in medicine on the horizon, he had more important things to think about.

His studies were at the top of the list. The first two years of medical school consisted of a rigorous curriculum of classroom instruction that required long hours and great concentration. Classes included gross anatomy, biochemistry, pathology, pharmacology, and other basic sciences. The program wasn't intended just to help the prospective doctors build a solid academic foundation, it was also designed to weed out those who weren't strong or disciplined enough to handle the work.

Thanks to his family background, Graham never had any trouble with the books. He was such a good student that he was easily able to tackle the rigors of classwork while taking the time to practice and play varsity baseball in the spring during his first year of medical school. Because his professors, the administration, and most of his peers at UNC were probably unaware of his dalliance with pro ball during the summer of 1902, it's likely that nobody questioned him about it. And even if they did know, it wouldn't have mattered. Most students took summer jobs to help finance their studies. Graham's job was simply a little more unconventional—and fun—than most.

When the North Carolina League's season came to a premature conclusion and the Hornets were disbanded, it was time to stop moonlighting and move on. Or so Graham thought.

Before he left home to return to school in Chapel Hill, word began to get around in baseball circles about a slender outfielder with pronounced eyebrows and quick feet who had come out of nowhere to star for those record-setting Hornets down in Charlotte. Graham's stock rose even higher in 1904 when he joined the Maryland baseball team. Though the individual records of that era have long been lost, Graham's presence in center field must have had a positive influence on the team, which went 10–4. Among the victories in a season described by the college's annual as having "achieved results which were never expected" was one over Graham's former team and undergraduate alma mater, the University of North Carolina.

For the first time, Graham's talents as an athlete were being noticed outside his home area. The scouts were impressed. So, in the summer of 1903, instead of returning home to Charlotte, where the North Carolina League was in a shambles and he had no guarantee of a place to play, he accepted an offer to go north to New Hampshire to play for Nashua of the Class B New England League. Graham got into 89 games that season, amassing 10 doubles, seven triples, and 30 stolen bases in 342 at-bats. Although he hit just .240, well below his norm, he still managed to make a name for himself with his speed and hustle. "Graham of Nashua is the fastest man in the league on a long spring," the July 19 edition of *Sporting Life* reported. "He easily makes two bases on many hits other men would count on but a single."

Whether it was Graham's speed, his potential at the plate, his strong throwing arm, or some other factor, Nashua's New England League rival Manchester saw enough in the young outfielder to trade for him late in the season. Manchester immediately invited him back to play again the following year. By that time, Graham had become completely intoxicated by the thrill of athletic competition. Things were going so well for him that he decided to expand his sporting horizons to the football field, once he followed his brother David's footsteps by transferring to Maryland to complete his medical training in Baltimore.

Although he had done no better than making the "scrub" team two years earlier at UNC, the older, more physically mature Graham proved good enough to make the Terrapins' varsity squad as a halfback. The quality of the team might also have had something to do with it. That fall, Maryland won just two of eight games under coach P. John Markey—beating Gallaudet, a school for the deaf, and Mount St. Mary's—while mustering a pair of scoreless ties, against Randolph-Macon and a group of soldiers from nearby Fort Monroe in Virginia.

Though not very successful as a collective effort, the 1903 football season was enjoyable for Graham. For one thing, he was under less pressure academically. Rather than spending his days in class and his evenings in the library working to memorize "the accepted truths" of his chosen science, as he

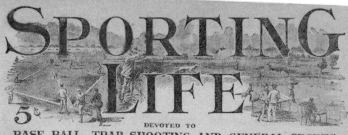

The cover of *Sporting Life* magazine of July 19, 1902, shows Graham with his Charlotte Hornets teammates, who had just broken a record with their 25-game winning streak. Moonlight is in the upper left corner.
COURTESY OF THE LA84 FOUNDATION

had at UNC, the third-year student was now concentrating mostly on clinical instruction and hands-on bedside care. He learned how to take blood pressures—a skill that would figure prominently in his future research—listen to the heart and lungs, and formulate diagnoses. Then he began using those skills on actual patients. The hospital work allowed Graham plenty of free time, so he spent his afternoons on the gridiron to fill the long months until the start of baseball season.

That didn't mean the medical faculty at Maryland was happy about his sporting endeavors. Many professors urged Graham to give up the games. When he respectfully turned down their requests, they appealed to the school's administration to force him to concentrate solely on his studies. But Dr. Robert Dorsey Coale, Maryland's popular dean and a man of sound judgment and unswerving integrity, wouldn't hear of it.

Playing football helped Graham get into the best physical condition of his life. Now 5-10½ and about 175 pounds, he breezed through his final collegiate season on the diamond before heading up to Massachusetts to play professional baseball. Yet even though he had sped through his remaining clinical studies, which allowed him to leave school early for the first and only time in his career to get a head start on the 1904 season, things didn't go well at first. On May 14, the *Lowell Courier* reported that Graham had "fallen off badly in hitting. He stands up to the plate with less confidence and swings weakly. All the teams are on the lookout for bunts when Graham goes to bat. No faster runner in the league, but a fast runner must have more than one trick up his sleeve." Eventually, he found his confidence and hitting stroke. In 437 at-bats over 108 games, the young moonlighter batted .272 with 15 doubles and 70 runs scored.

GRAHAM, ARCHIBALD W.   Charlotte, N. C.

"The world knows nothing of its greatest men."

Age 25, Wt. 169, Ht. 5.10. Class secretary '04-
'05, Varsity football '03-'04, Varsity baseball
'03-'04—'04-'05, A. B. University of N. C. '01.

Graham's entry in the 1905 University of Maryland annual
COURTESY OF THE UNIVERSITY OF MARYLAND

His defensive skills and savvy were among the best in the league, as displayed on August 23 when he participated in one of the most unusual triple plays in baseball history. All nine of Manchester's players touched the ball before the three runners were put out. Graham, who was playing center field at the time, moved in to cover second during a rundown. He helped record the second out on a runner trapped between second and third.

Because of plays such as that, Manchester's management decided to ask him back again in 1905. But Graham wouldn't return to the New England League anymore. He was a young man with plenty of options when he packed his belongings at the end of the 1904 season. He was almost 25 (though some believe he lied about his age to make himself more attractive to baseball scouts), he was heading back to Maryland to complete his medical degree, and he was already fielding internship offers from several prominent hospitals. On the diamond, he was being courted by no fewer than three major league teams. He was no longer just a med student who happened to be moonlighting as a baseball player. When the New York Giants bought his contract from Manchester on September 25, 1904, and invited him to join the team the next spring, he officially became a baseball player who happened to be moonlighting as a med student.

CHAPTER 3

Fifteen Minutes in the Sun
The Big Game

———

*"We just don't recognize the most significant
moments in our lives when they were happening.
Back then, I thought there'd be other days. I didn't
realize that was the only day."*

MOONLIGHT GRAHAM IN
THE NOVEL *SHOELESS JOE*

MOONLIGHT GRAHAM'S "ONLY DAY" in the majors began the
same way every other day had since his activation by the New
York Giants three weeks earlier—sitting in the dugout watching his teammates destroy the competition. At least he had
the best seat in the house. And it wasn't an easy seat to get.

The Giants were the preeminent team in the National
League at the time, having won the 1904 pennant by a whop-
ping 13 games. They would have been a heavy favorite to win
the World Series that year had they not refused to meet the
Boston Americans because team ownership determined that
the rules of play were too haphazardly defined. It was the only

time until the players' strike of 1994 that a World Series was canceled.

The Giants were even more dominant the following season. Under the leadership of Hall of Fame manager John McGraw, the New Yorkers went 105–48 in 1905 and won the National League by nine games over second-place Pittsburgh. This time, inspired by criticism from both fans and writers, they agreed to participate in the postseason. They went on to win the first of McGraw's three World Series championships by outscoring Connie Mack's Philadelphia Athletics 15–3 in the five-game series, with all four of their wins coming by shutouts.

Though New York's dominance was built around a pitching staff that included 20-game winners Christy Matthewson, Joe McGinnity, and Red Ames, the Giants also fielded a formidable lineup that outscored the opposition by nearly 300 runs and led the league in both scoring and stolen bases. Unlike today's managers, who rely heavily on their benches to help get their teams through the rigors of a long season, McGraw rarely deviated from his everyday lineup. Other than the eight regular position players, only three Giants saw significant action in 1905. One of those, 36-year-old reserve catcher and first baseman Boileryard Clarke, batted just 50 times in 31 games.

The outfield was especially talented. Center fielder Mike Donlin hit .356 with seven homers and 80 RBIs, left fielder Sam Mertes hit .279 and drove in 108 runs, and right fielder George Browne batted .293. Their prowess made it difficult for a newly arrived rookie to get much playing time. It also didn't help that the left-handed-hitting Graham was both a privileged 27-year-old college boy with other career aspirations and a Southerner, two things that likely rubbed McGraw the wrong way.

Known as "Little Napoleon" to his fans and "Mugsy" to his many enemies, McGraw was a difficult man to get along with even under the best of circumstances. As a third baseman with the old Baltimore Orioles, St. Louis Cardinals, and Giants, he had never hesitated to fight anyone, even his teammates. As a manager, he won more games than he did friends because of his disagreeable personality and dictatorial style.

For McGraw, baseball was a saving grace from a life that almost certainly would have landed him in prison or worse. His childhood was marred by an abusive father—a Union soldier during the Civil War—and frequent brushes with the law. McGraw's hatred for authority and authority figures never faded. It eventually led him into frequent skirmishes with both umpires and American League president Ban Johnson.

McGraw never thought twice about stepping on people, no matter how insignificant, if they got in his path or rubbed him the wrong way. In 1906, for instance, he was arrested in Pittsburgh and held on the then-princely sum of $500 bail for allegedly assaulting a 13-year-old boy as he left the ballpark following a game. The boy, named Brady, was among a crowd of youngsters hooting and jeering as the Giants made their way from the stadium to their bus. McGraw took exception to their comments. Never one to let a good fight pass him by, he took a swipe with his hand, catching the boy across the face. The charges were dropped the next day when the youngster appeared before the magistrate with no marks on his face.

As surly as he could be, McGraw had a soft spot for those who shared his single-minded dedication to baseball and gave their all for the game. He remained amazingly loyal to them, even when they made the worst of mistakes. The most famous example of this was when he gave Fred Merkle a raise despite his infamous base-running blunder that cost the Giants the 1908 pennant. On the other hand, if McGraw didn't like a player or thought he wasn't dedicated to the team, the fiery skipper could be unmerciful. "Don't ever talk to me," he once allegedly told a player. "I speak to you and you just shut up."

Chances are he had little use for Graham, the son of a Confederate veteran and a player who, in McGraw's mind, wasn't dedicated enough to report to spring training on time. Or worse, a player who might be planning to leave the team early, in the heat of a pennant race, even for as good a reason as completing medical school or starting an internship. Complicating matters was the fact that Graham wasn't completely healthy when he got to New York. Still hobbling from a leg injury suffered the previous fall at the University of Maryland while playing football, he wasn't able to show off the speed that had helped him get to the majors, as reported by *Sporting Life* in October 1904. "He will be a revelation to the habituates of the Polo Grounds," the magazine proclaimed. "He ought to hold his job by his feet, as it were." Graham was so fast that two seasons after he left Manchester, he was still the standard to which others were compared. Tom Burke, an outfielder for Lynn of the New England League, was said to be "a sprinter of the Archie Graham type."

Because of McGraw's combative reputation and his own shy nature and mannered Southern upbringing, it is doubtful that Graham ever approached his manager to ask when he might play. Instead, he sat close by on the bench, quietly watching and waiting for an opportunity he hoped would soon come. "I got a great chance to sit beside John McGraw during that season with the Giants," Graham recalled in a 1963 interview with the *Charlotte News*. "And [I] learned a lot of baseball from the old man."

His baseball education continued on the afternoon of June 29 at Brooklyn's Washington Park.

*This is the only known picture of Moonlight Graham practicing in a
Giants uniform during his short stay with the team.*
COURTESY OF THE LYNN WILLIAMSON DIDIER COLLECTION

Mal Eason was on the mound for the last-place Superbas, as the Brooklyn team was then known. It wasn't long before it became obvious that he would be no match for the Giants' heavy hitters. In the top of the second, Billy Gilbert singled home Bill Dahlen for the first run of the game. The next inning, the Giants broke the game open by scoring six times, highlighted by a three-run homer off the bat of first baseman Dan McGann and a triple by catcher Frank Bowerman.

With Matthewson on the mound pitching well, New York's eighth straight win was already a formality when McGraw stepped out of character and did the unthinkable. He started clearing his bench in the bottom of the fifth. First, he replaced McGann with Sammy Strang. Then, after the Giants scored three more times in the sixth to increase the lead to 10–0, he sent Boileryard Clarke in for Bowerman and seldom-used Claude Elliott onto the mound for Matthewson to start the sixth. In the corner of the dugout, young Graham perked up with anticipation upon the rash of substitutions. But after the seventh inning came and went without any further changes, his excitement was undoubtedly tempered by the realization that he might not get in. Again.

Then it happened. As he watched his Giants head back to their positions for the bottom of the eighth, Graham was startled by the sight of McGraw standing in front of him pointing a "bony finger" in his direction. Not one for unnecessary small talk, especially during a game, the old man uttered just two simple words: "Right field."

That was all the excited rookie needed to hear. "I jumped up like I was sitting on a spring, grabbed my glove and trotted out, hoping I wouldn't trip or do anything to attract attention to me," W. P. Kinsella's fictionalized Graham says in *Shoeless Joe.* The public address announcer boomed out his name in a voice that echoed all around the empty grandstand. "Graham, now playing right field," he said. But Graham himself didn't hear it. He was too focused to notice.

He probably didn't hear the roar of the crowd either. That's because it's doubtful many of the 2,000 in attendance were still around by the time Graham began what the *New York Telegram* called his "two joyous innings in the right garden." Of those faithful who remained in the stands, few knew, let alone cared, who Graham was. But it didn't matter. Whatever happened from that point on, Moonlight Graham could always say he was a major leaguer.

Even so, he couldn't help feeling a little overwhelmed by the enormity of the moment and the cavernous Brooklyn ballpark. His mind might even have wandered back to that early minor league game in Charlotte three years earlier when he had been so nervous about facing a veteran pitcher that he had to be shoved into the batter's box by his manager.

"I practiced in the outfield all the time I'd been with the Giants, but it was a different matter to play it," the literary Graham relates in *Shoeless Joe.* "It seemed like a mile from the infield, the batter looked like a midget, his bat a toothpick. I tried to take deep breaths and calm down, wondering what I'd do if the ball was hit my way, hoping it wouldn't be, and at the same time hoping it would. I tried to make myself extra alert, watch the bat, the pitcher's motion so I could get a good jump on the ball. But I felt so isolated."

Boasting a seating capacity of 18,800, Washington Park was a bit more spacious than the Giants' home across the river in Manhattan, the original Polo Grounds. Compared to the minor league stadiums in which Graham had played the three previous seasons, it must have seemed enormous. A 42-foot-high brick wall that protected the right-field line only 300 feet away from home plate made the place feel even more imposing. A century later, a portion of Washington Park still stands as part of the Third Avenue wall to the Con Edison yard in Brooklyn. It is the oldest major league structure still standing, predating both Chicago's Wrigley Field and Boston's Fenway Park.

If Washington Park made Graham feel small and isolated, the Superbas didn't do anything to help him feel less detached on that glorious afternoon in June 1905. They went out in order in the bottom of the eighth, a pair of Elliott strikeouts sandwiched around John Dobbs's lazy fly out to Mike Donlin in center.

Then came the ninth. Batting in George Browne's leadoff spot, Graham needed two men ahead of him to reach base for a crack at batting in the majors. His chances didn't look good when Art Devlin popped to short and Billy Gilbert fanned against Brooklyn reliever Jack Doscher for two quick outs. But Clarke homered to left-center to give the Giants an 11–0 lead and keep Graham's chances alive.

Had the score been closer, McGraw might have elected to pinch-hit for his pitcher. Not this time. Given the big lead and the disdain managers of that era had for using their bullpens, McGraw allowed Elliott to grab a bat and head to the plate as scheduled. In the dugout, Graham remained hopeful as he picked out a bat and took a deep breath and a couple of practice chops before strolling out to the on-deck circle. There, he watched helplessly as Elliott ended the inning with a popup to second.

Not yet realizing that his only opportunity to hit had just passed him by, Graham retrieved his glove and returned to right field without emotion. It wasn't until years later, after he had plenty of time to reflect on the moment, that the disappointment of coming so close to his dream without realizing it started to set in. Once it did, Graham began telling people, including a reporter from his hometown *Charlotte News,* that

New York Giants manager John "Mugsy" McGraw, an old-school baseball man who had little use for a college boy like Graham.
COURTESY OF THE ASSOCIATED PRESS

he'd actually batted once, drawing a walk, before suffering a season-ending broken leg attempting to steal second. All available records and play-by-play accounts of the game disprove that claim.

What isn't as certain is whether or not Graham got to handle a live ball defensively during the bottom of the ninth. The records aren't clear. But it's entirely possible that the nervous rookie had to make plays on as many as two Brooklyn hits. The more likely chance would have come off the bat of Harry Lumley, a left-handed pull hitter who singled to start the inning against the right-handed Elliott. Two batters later, after Lumley stole second, switch hitter Charlie Malay also singled. The fact that Lumley was held at third, however, suggests that the ball either didn't leave the infield or fell in just in front of the left fielder.

Lumley eventually scored the Superbas' only run on a bases-loaded walk to Lou Ritter. Elliott escaped further damage by striking out Bill Bergen to end the game. And just like that, the "only day" of Moonlight Graham's major league career was over. He remained with the Giants for another week, sitting close by McGraw, waiting for another chance that never came. New York went 4–2 against Brooklyn and Philadelphia during that stretch.

Finally, after a 9–7 victory over the Phillies in Philadelphia on July 5, McGraw decided to make a move. This time, instead of putting Graham in a game, he shipped him out to the minors. A one-sentence item in *Sporting Life* magazine the following day was his epitaph with the Giants: "Archie Graham, an extra outfielder of the New York Giants, has been sold by McGraw to the Scranton club." Already a journeyman accustomed to such transactions, Graham quietly packed his belongings, boarded the train for the two-and-a-half-hour ride to Scranton, and reported to his new assignment.

CHAPTER 4

Majoring in the Minors
A Giant in Scranton

---

*"Graham, an outfielder of the New York Giants,
comes with a great reputation as a base stealer
and sticker. Last year he batted .278 in the New
England League and fielded at a .910 clip."*
ITEM IN THE *SCRANTON TIMES*, JULY 5, 1905

MOONLIGHT GRAHAM WOUND UP SIGNING with the Giants
over Brooklyn and the Boston Red Sox primarily because he
fancied the idea of playing for fiery manager John McGraw.
It also didn't hurt that the Giants' Upper West Side address
was the most convenient to New York's Postgraduate Hospital, where Graham had spent the winter caring for patients
and doing research as part of his medical internship. From
an emotional and practical standpoint, his decision was a
prudent one. But as a baseball player with designs on getting
back to the major leagues, and quickly, he would have been
much better off joining Brooklyn or the Red Sox, teams whose

lineups would have been much less difficult to crack than that of the talent-laden Giants.

He began to understand that cruel reality almost immediately upon his arrival at the Polo Grounds once he graduated from Maryland in early June. As much respect and admiration as he had for McGraw, the feeling was hardly mutual. It took just four weeks and that now-famous cameo appearance against Brooklyn for old Mugsy to grow tired of seeing Graham take up space on his bench and put him on a train bound for Scranton.

The idea was for Graham to go down to the minors and play his way into shape, since he had missed all of spring training and the first two months of the season while finishing his studies. By mid-August, the newspapers in both New York and Scranton reported that McGraw was clamoring for the moonlighting doctor to return to the Giants once the New York State League season was completed.

As disappointed as he was with the demotion, getting sent to the minors was hardly a slap in the face for a player of Graham's experience. Only 16 major league teams existed at the time, and because rosters were made up of 18 players, compared to the 25-man units used in modern times, far fewer opportunities were available at baseball's highest level. That made the competition in the minors nearly as fierce, if not more so, than in the so-called big-time. In fact, many lesser leagues bristled at the name *minor* and refused to use it when referring to their product. They believed that the quality of baseball being played by their teams was equal or superior to that in New York, Boston, Cleveland, and other major cities. In many cases, a top minor leaguer playing for a financially solvent team could make more money than if he were the last man sitting at the end of the bench for McGraw's Giants.

It was a common practice for minor league teams to challenge their major league counterparts to midseason exhibition games, and they took great pleasure when they managed to beat their more-publicized rivals. Although the big leaguers rarely used their regular lineups, the hastily arranged contests always drew big crowds and generated large sums of money for team owners. The minor league players also benefited from their direct exposure to the managers and scouts who accompanied the major leaguers. A strong performance might earn them a contract or an invitation to spring training the following year.

Graham didn't have to concern himself with any of that. He was already the property of the Giants. And Scranton was hardly the bushes. The central Pennsylvania town was a thriving industrial center in the early part of the 20th century. And like most places in the days before professional football and basketball began to get off the ground, it had a healthy affinity for baseball. The Miners were members of the New York State League, whose Class B designation was the equivalent to today's Class AA level.

Such classifications, however, carried far less significance in those days. The reason was that no direct affiliations existed between major and minor league clubs as they do today. Such a practice did not become commonplace until Branch Rickey established baseball's first farm system with the St. Louis Cardinals in 1931. Until then, major league teams sold or loaned the contracts of their surplus players to whatever minor league club was available. Whenever possible, considerations such as location, potential playing time, and previous relationships with teammates or managers were taken into account. That's probably why the Giants chose to send Graham to Scranton and manager Eddie Ashenback, rather

NAME Graham A. W. "Archie" Manchester

LEAGUE New England

CLASS D CLUB Manchester

RELEASE PURCHASED

DATE	CLUB

RESERVED

DATE	CLUB
10/18/04	Manchester
9/20/05	New York
1/25/05	Boston Amer.
9/26/06	Scranton

RELEASE

DATE	CLUB

CASH RECEIVED

Date	First Payment	Second Payment	Date
10/21/04	90 Scranton		

DRAFTED

Date	CLUB
9/25/04	New York
9/20/10	Cleveland to Boston A.L.

CASH PAID

Date	First Payment	Date	Second Payment

AWARDED

CLAIMED

REMARKS 5/31/05 Second payment of draft from Manchester Clu.
See Dec # 180.

Card kept on file at the Hall of Fame chronicling the movement of Doc Graham's contract
COURTESY OF THE NATIONAL BASEBALL HALL OF FAME AND MUSEUM

than somewhere in the highest designation of the minors, such as the Class A Southern Association.

The blow of being sent back to the minors was softened upon Graham's arrival in Pennsylvania, where he was greeted at the train station by a familiar, sympathetic face. A veteran baseball man who had coached Graham in college and signed him to his first professional contract in Charlotte three years earlier, Ashenback had been hired to replace Jimmy Garry only a few weeks earlier. The Miners were 19–36 and solidly entrenched in the basement of the eight-team league by the time Graham reported. On July 7, the new skipper penciled his new player and old friend into the leadoff spot for both games of a doubleheader against the first-place Jags of Amsterdam-Johnstown-Gloversville.

"Graham comes with a great reputation as a base stealer and sticker," the *Scranton Times* reported that day. After Graham picked up a hit and helped the Miners gain a split of his first two games, the newspaper proclaimed that both he and teammate Arthur Spooner, who had been brought in to play first base, "showed up well." Maybe Graham showed up too well, because after collecting 14 hits in his first eight games with Scranton, he was approached by a representative of the outlaw Tri-State League. The man told him that if he jumped his contract to play for a team in nearby Altoona, Pennsylvania, he could make much more than the $225 a month Ashenback was giving him.

Under today's rules, Graham would never have even thought about making such a move. It simply wouldn't be allowed. But organized baseball was still in its infancy during the first decade of the 20th century. The minor leagues were a patchwork of independent teams scattered across the landscape, playing by different rules and beholden to nothing more than their own bottom line. The designation *minor league* wasn't officially used to describe teams outside of the National League and the American League. It was coined by big-city sportswriters and wasn't universally adopted until years later.

Because teams in New York, Chicago, Philadelphia, and Boston generated more money and thus could afford larger stadiums, generally better pay, and nicer accommodations than teams in other towns, the best players naturally gravitated toward them. When they did, their former teams in smaller towns were left high and dry. It was a system that concerned league owners so much that in 1901, Eastern League president Patrick T. Powers decided it had to be changed. Rather than trying to compete directly with the more powerful National League and American League, he decided to form an association of smaller entities with a standard set of rules governing officiating, player drafts, contracts, and the location of teams. Fourteen leagues, including the New York State League, agreed to join what became known as the National Association of Professional Baseball Leagues. The new alliance became a financial savior for many of its members, in that it prevented players from jumping from league to league and required monetary compensation for players moving up to the majors.

The problem was that not everybody signed on, leaving numerous outlaw, semipro, mill, and town leagues that were not bound by the same rules and restrictions. In many cases, these leagues—which became known as "bush leagues"—were disorganized and run by unscrupulous owners who cared little for written contracts and often reneged on their promises of more pay, playing time, and other perks. None of that seemed to matter to Graham, who despite his intellect never had much sense for the dollar. Figuring that one minor league team was as good as another—especially when the one he was on was mired so deeply in last place—he accepted the offer from Altoona and quietly left town.

Graham's official reason for departing Scranton was a moral objection to playing ball on Sundays. Never mind that he wasn't a religious man or that he hadn't bothered to tell anyone about his problem with playing on Sundays until just before he left. After all he'd been through with McGraw and the Giants, he was suddenly in demand again, and when he saw an opportunity to take the money and run, he did exactly that. It didn't take him long to learn that money doesn't always buy happiness. After just three days in Altoona, Graham realized that his new teammates weren't much better than the Miners and that the Tri-State League was nowhere near as professional as the New York State League. So he decided to get out. But getting out of Altoona proved much more difficult than getting in.

The odyssey actually began in nearby Johnstown, where Graham's team had just played a game. When Ashenback showed up to retrieve his star player, he was met by an angry mob of fans and teammates who weren't about to let the former major leaguer go without a fight. Fearing that the crowd would try to kidnap Graham and hold him against his will, Ashenback snuck him out the back door under cover of darkness and made a run for it. Literally. Instead of going straight to the train depot, they set out on a trek that the *Scranton Times* described as "a cross-country walk of 10 miles to a little place called Steward," where they caught the train and went on to join their team in Albany, New York. "Doc," the newspaper said upon his return, "has been missed."

The same couldn't be said for everyone on that 1905 Miners team. Spooner, the big first baseman who had come to Scranton along with Graham, was released on July 17, making him the first of Eddie Ashenback's players—and the second first baseman—to be cut since the new manager took over. Spooner's dismissal started a parade of potential first sackers. John Gaughan, a heavy-hitting kid from the Scranton amateur league, was signed next, thanks to the not-so-subtle backing of the local newspaper. But he was clearly in over his head and lasted only one game. Then came veteran Ed McGamwell, who like Graham had started the season in the major leagues, with Brooklyn. When McGamwell injured his hand, a player named Conkling was signed, followed by another local player, Kane, until McGamwell finally returned in late August.

First base was hardly the only tinkering done to the Scranton roster. Desperately searching for the right combination, Ashenback went through players like George Steinbrenner would go through managers during his early days as owner of the New York Yankees nearly 70 years later. Some of the new men proved to be keepers, such as young Joe Schrall in center field and John Pugh, the new third baseman. Others, however, didn't stay around long enough for the fans to learn their names.

For most of the summer, nothing seemed to work. On August 1, with a chance to catch and pass Binghamton for seventh place, the Miners dropped a doubleheader to the Bingoes to fall to 32–53. Things got so frustrating in the final innings of a 7–3 loss in the nightcap that Ashenback, an old outfielder, even inserted himself into the game on the mound to pitch. "The cry 'wait until next year' is a long, long way off," the *Scranton Times* reported the following day. "Binghamton is playing fine ball now and is bound to climb. Scranton figured on passing [manager Robert] Drury's men once, but we were way off in our mathematics."

While the number in the win column clearly wasn't rising fast enough for Ashenback, his team, and the local media, it didn't seem to matter much to the fans of Scranton. A hardy blue-collar lot, many of whom were actual miners, they came right to the ballpark from their jobs, still wearing their tin helmets with lamps on them. They seemed happy just to have the distraction of a ball club they could call their own. Scranton far and away led the league in attendance, its figures dwarfing those of its neighboring rival in Wilkes-Barre, whose more accomplished team played in a much bigger stadium than the Miners' Athletic Park.

The phenomenon didn't go unnoticed by George M. Graham, sporting editor of the *Philadelphia North American.* In his column on August 7, Graham wrote that Scranton presented the novel baseball spectacle of a town that loyally supported a loser: "Since the city entered a team in the New York State League, it has not had the pleasure of seeing its name high in the standing, but this has made no difference to Scranton. The team was a local institution; it has been started by men who loved the game and were cheerfully ready to bear the financial loss, should any occur; hence the club must be supported heartily in victory or in defeat, and so it has. Such fealty deserves its recognition, and it is bound to come. The team is in the hands of men who will eventually put it on a winning basis and the time is not far distant."

As it turned out, the promised improvement was closer than anyone—including team owners J. W. Barnes and E. J. Coleman—ever imagined. Starting on August 7, the day George Graham's column appeared in the Philadelphia paper, the Miners suddenly hit on a winning combination. Their turnaround started with a 3–0 defeat of league-leading A.J. & G., in which Doc Graham, as he was now known, "batted strong, having three safe cracks." Two days later, Scranton swept a doubleheader from the Jags on a pair of shutouts despite scoring just three runs combined. In the opener, Graham scored the game's only run in the bottom of the first after singling, stealing second, going to third on a ground out, and scoring on Joe Schrall's hit. In the nightcap, he showed off his superior speed by executing a double steal with second baseman Eddie Shortell to set up one run, then scored the second in a 2–0 victory after stretching a long single into a double in the eighth.

For the first time all season, the Miners were playing consistently good ball and finding ways to win games. They caught Binghamton and escaped the cellar on August 20 when they pounded out an 11–0 win over Troy and the Bingoes lost 3–2 to A.J. & G. "It's like wearing a new coat, getting out of last place," the local paper proclaimed.

Once they put it on, Ashenback and his crew had no intention of taking that new coat off. They took three more from Troy—including an 8–1 win highlighted by three more hits by Graham—and in the process passed the Trojans for sixth place. The winning streak finally ended at seven with a 4–1 loss to Binghamton in the first game of a doubleheader on August 26. But the Miners bounced right back to win six more in a row, their eyes now set on passing Utica for fifth and the possibility of a first-division finish. Not even a false rumor that Graham had been traded to Syracuse for a pitcher, reported in the *Syracuse Journal* on September 2, could derail the Scranton express. During the month of August, the team won 21 games, lost 10, and tied one.

The Miners were rewarded for their efforts when they arrived home from an extended road trip and were greeted by a league-record crowd of 7,500 for a Labor Day game against archrival Wilkes-Barre. With McGamwell healthy again and back in the lineup, the Miners pounded out a 7–1 victory that left the excited fans wondering what might have happened had the big first baseman been able to play all year.

Things were going so well that the *Scranton Times* reported that "McGraw is already clamoring for the doctor" and suggested that Graham would be back in New York once the minor league season ended. But that's not what happened. Instead, the final few games of the 1905 season proved to be an anticlimax, especially for Graham. After his team lost both ends of a doubleheader to Syracuse the following day, he packed his bat and glove, said goodbye to Ashenback and his teammates—who still had five more games to play—and headed to Baltimore to spend the winter doing postgraduate work in pathology at Johns Hopkins University. As much fun as playing in Scranton had been that summer, he had no plans to return.

What Graham didn't know was that his contract spent the winter being used as a bargaining chip in a dispute between the Giants and Boston Red Sox owner John I. Taylor. The drama began when Graham's name was left off New York's postseason reserve list, either by accident or by McGraw's design. That left him vulnerable to be "drafted" by any other major league team. And that's what Boston did. But Taylor's attempt to steal Graham hit a snag because the Giants still owed the doctor money. Although the Red Sox owner would "insist upon getting the man," as reported by *Sporting Life*, a deal was eventually worked out to allow Graham to stay with the Giants—temporarily, at least.

Oblivious to it all, and finally free from the burden of medical school, Graham attended spring training for the first time in his career. He was confident he would make the Giants' roster and be patrolling right field at the Polo Grounds on opening day in 1906. Maybe he showed up too confident. Either that or McGraw still had a negative opinion of him from the year before and didn't feel like giving him a fair chance to show what he could do. Whatever the case, Graham was sent to Memphis of the Class A Southern Association while the rest of the team headed north to New York.

Stunned, the baseball-playing doctor refused to report to his minor league assignment. He eventually changed his mind, but his heart wasn't in it. He lasted just 12 games, picking up 11 hits in 42 at bats, before the Giants cut their losses and sent him on his way. As far as Graham was concerned, it was just as well. If he couldn't play for the Giants or anyone else in the majors, he preferred to return to Scranton, where he knew and respected the manager, was appreciated by the fans, and had a legitimate shot at winning a pennant, even if it was a step down from the Southern Association on the minor league ladder. He got to town just in time for the season opener against defending champion A.J. & G.

The team to which Graham returned looked a lot like the one that had finished the previous season as the hottest in the New York State League. Among the other returnees were center fielder Schrall, second baseman Shortell, right fielder Fred Betts, shortstop Gus Ziemer, and pitcher Larry Hanifan. With the addition of first baseman Bud Sharpe and third baseman Heine Krug, both of whom would go on to play in the majors at the end of the season, it was as obvious as their slick new black, blue, and gray uniforms that this group of Miners had the look of a winner. On the eve of the first game, Jags manager Howard Earl said in the *Scranton Times* that he thought highly of the newly assembled Scranton squad. "He sees no reason why the team should not assume a good position in the league race," the newspaper wrote.

It didn't take long for others to see what Earl did in the Miners. Despite teeth-chattering temperatures hovering around the freezing point, and inspired by an opening-day appearance by Mayor J. B. Dimmick and a spirited rebel yell by their manager, they took three of four from the Jags in the season's first series. Even then, Ashenback wasn't satisfied. First, he "laid off" Hanifan. Then he dealt Betts—who was off to a slow start with the bat—to Albany. Neither move was popular. But after the Miners returned home from a two-week road trip with an 11–5 record and a solid second-place standing behind league-leading Binghamton, no one was prepared to question Ashenback's judgment anymore.

In fact, perhaps sensing something special was happening, the fans of Scranton turned out in record numbers for the team's first game back, against Wilkes-Barre on May 30. The grandstand and bleachers were jammed more than an hour before game time, forcing those arriving later to pour onto the field. Team officials, unwilling to turn away ticket buyers, sent a call to city hall for more police to control the mob and keep the peace. With the help of the players, the newly bolstered security force succeeded in clearing enough space on the diamond for the game to be played. To ensure that the crowd of nearly 8,000 didn't interfere with the action, the teams agreed on special ground rules that allowed for two bases on any ball hit into the crowd and one base on an overthrow. "Yesterday afternoon was the greatest day in the history of the Athletic Park," was how the *Scranton Times* described the scene.

The day got even better when the home team scored seven times in the bottom of the sixth to overcome a 6–3 deficit and beat the Barons 13–8. Graham contributed by singling home a run in the big sixth and sending a double into the crowd in right to drive home another in the bottom of the seventh.

He added a two-run triple a day later in a 9–3 win that pulled Scranton even with Binghamton heading into a three-game weekend series with the Bingoes that would turn into a mismatch. Three straight decisive wins, followed by a sweep of Syracuse, catapulted the Miners into first place. They stretched their lead to four and a half games on June 8 when Troy finally figured out a way to beat them, ending an 11-game winning streak. By that time, it was painfully clear to the rest of the New York State League that there was no stopping Ashenback's boys.

In Scranton, already a booming mining town with a lot going for it, enthusiasm and civic pride were at an all-time high. "Little else is talked about in the mine, the mills, shops and factories," the local paper reported. "The ardent wish of all is for the success of the team and on all sides can be heard words of praise for the successful management of Ashenback."

The problem was that others outside the Wyoming Valley were also starting to take notice. Harrisburg of the outlaw Tri-State League came calling first, encouraging the Scranton manager to jump ship by offering considerably more than the $500 being paid to the current Harrisburg skipper. A few days later, a sports column in *The Medler,* a weekend publication in Ashenback's hometown of Cincinnati, suggested that he would be a popular replacement should the struggling Reds decided to make a change. But the Miners' manager wasn't going anywhere, at least until the season was over.

Seeing a championship there for the taking, he wasn't about to let his good players get away either. The one exception was Schrall, the promising young right fielder who entered the season with an understanding that he would be allowed to leave for Wheeling anytime the Central League decided to recall him. That happened in early June, about the time Scranton was starting to catch fire. Because of the timing of Schrall's departure and the less-than-professional tactics employed by a number of rival leagues, concern began to spread among fans at the Athletic Park that other player defections might follow. Most of the gossip surrounded the possible sale of third baseman Heine Krug and first baseman Bud Sharpe. In an effort to head off the rumors before they became a distraction, Ashenback fired a preemptive strike by calling them "an insult to my intelligence" in an open letter to fans in the local newspaper.

Having successfully defused one potential crisis, the wily manager was able to turn his attention back to the diamond, where he faced another problem. It happened late in a 4–2 victory over Troy on June 7, the final contest of the 11-game winning streak, when Graham came down awkwardly while chasing a fly ball in left field. His ankle began to swell immediately. Although he was able to finish the game, the injury prevented him from playing again for more than a week. But his teammates never missed a beat in his absence, winning seven of nine games and increasing their lead over Binghamton.

If Graham was beginning to worry that he might be expendable, he need not have. After only his fourth game away, the *Scranton Times* reported that "it seems lonesome without Doc Graham in the lineup." Still, he must have felt just a little threatened. Either that or he wasn't accustomed to the inactivity his injury forced upon him. Whatever the reason, the Miners' leadoff man decided to come back before his ankle was fully healed. He rejoined the team in Albany and lasted just one at-bat before hobbling back to the dugout in pain. When Graham sat out the next day's game, the *Times* worried that the bum ankle "may prove his undoing." The newspaper's concern held a bit of truth. Because Graham's game was built around speed, a serious leg injury could well have proven career threatening. This one wasn't.

Back in left field against Syracuse on June 21, Graham showed he still had plenty of life in his legs by hustling out a double in four trips in a 5–0 Scranton win. But just as he was getting back onto his feet, his team began to stumble for the first time all season. A loss to Syracuse followed by a three-game sweep at the hands of A.J. & G. might have been cause for panic had Scranton not built a commanding eight-and-a-half-game cushion over the rest of the league.

The Miners continued to sleepwalk through the next three weeks. Not all of their woes were self-inflicted. On one occasion, their train was delayed twice—once by mechanical problems and once by an accident on the tracks ahead of them—forcing their late arrival for a game at Troy. The game was originally ruled a forfeit because they weren't there for the scheduled starting time. That decision was eventually reversed. After considerable and heated discussion, the game finally began, only to be called after seven innings because of darkness with the score tied 4–4. At least it wasn't a loss.

Even with their big lead, the Miners were in desperate need of a cure for their doldrums. It was a good thing they had a licensed doctor on call at the top of their batting order. Hitting just below the .300 mark when he stepped to the plate against the Jags on July 17, Graham took matters into his own hands and ignited the spark that would carry his team through the rest of the season. His 4-for-5 performance, which included a double and a triple, catapulted Scranton to a 4–2 win and began a torrid stretch in which he amassed 13 hits in his next 33 at-bats.

Coinciding with Graham's rapid rise among the league's hitting leaders was the Miners' return to the form that had helped them establish their dominance during the first two months of the season. Strengthened by the return of Hanifan on the mound and the addition of Hogan Yancey, a big, well-built Canadian from Toronto of the Eastern League, the team took off again. As the heat of July melted into the dog days of August, Scranton stood a full 13 games ahead of A.J. & G. with a record of 54–25.

If the defending champions had any realistic hope of catching Ashenback's nine, or at the very least making the race a little more respectable, their best opportunity came in a three-game series with the Miners at the Athletic Park starting on August 13. The big series, however, turned out to be nothing more than another showcase for the powerful Scranton squad and its fleet-footed left fielder determined to show he was still a hitter of major league ability. "Graham again proved he is the real thing when he takes to swatting the pill," the *Scranton Times* reported after a 5–0 Miners win in the opener, in which the former Giant went 3 for 4 with a double and his second home run of the season. The homer was more a display of speed than power, as his low line drive found its way behind the billboards in center field and he circled the bases before it could be retrieved. In game two, Graham went 2 for 2 with a stolen base, a run, two RBIs, and two sacrifices in an 8–2 Scranton victory that, in the estimation of the local newspaper, all but wrapped up the league crown. "With everyone on the job and all hands working like beavers," the *Times* wrote, "the pennant sure does loom up pretty close." Although the reeling Jags salvaged a little pride by winning the finale 8–4, Graham did his part with three more hits, giving him eight in 10 official at-bats in the series. In all, he produced a homer, a double, four runs, four RBIs, and three stolen bases.

Now, instead of just helping his team win and trying to impress old Mugsy McGraw enough to earn a recall to New York, Graham found himself with a new motivation for the final month of the 1906 season. With his average soaring to .322, second only to Art Weaver of the Jags, he now began to set his sights on winning the league batting title as well. It was a goal that kept him sharp and focused while others around him began falling victim to complacency, injury, and distractions, such as the publicity stunt on September 1 that had former heavyweight boxing champion James J. Corbett playing first base for six innings in a game against Wilkes-Barre.

The Miners were 80–41 when they clinched the New York State League pennant on September 7. They then proceeded to lose seven straight. Ashenback earned partial blame for the skid by trying out several local amateurs on the mound. The losing streak certainly wasn't Graham's fault. Through it all, he continued to hit. On September 11, his two-run single capped a four-run ninth-inning rally that beat Syracuse 4–2. On September 18, he amassed three hits in a loss to Albany. He finished his surge with three more hits in a victory against Wilkes-Barre on September 21, giving him 31 in his final 80 at-bats of the season. His .335 average left him tied with Weaver for the league crown. Because Graham's percentage was slightly higher when factored to the next decimal, he was declared the champion.

But that wasn't even the best news.

With the help of his longtime ally Ashenback, who arranged an exhibition game against the Giants in Scranton the day after the season ended, Graham finally got the chance to show McGraw that he was worthy of another shot at playing in the majors. Certainly, he could make a much more convincing argument in person, on the field, than he could by handing the old man an impressive stat sheet from some third-rate minor league. At least that's what he thought. What Graham didn't know was that McGraw probably wasn't watching very closely that afternoon. Having already signed A.J. & G.'s young right fielder, a kid named Joe Birmingham, to finish out the season in New York, McGraw had already moved on and had no more use for the moonlighting doctor.

To his credit, Doc accomplished exactly what he set out to do in the game. After nervously striking out in his first at-bat, the Miners' left fielder finished the day with a walk, a double, and an RBI single in four official trips to the plate. Scranton won the game 9–1, to the delight of the 6,000-plus hometown fans in attendance. Never mind that the accomplishment was lessened considerably by the fact that only a handful of starters were in the Giants' lineup, and that the Matthewson who came out of the bullpen to pitch wasn't future Hall of Famer Christy—a Scranton native—but his less-talented kid brother, Henry.

Vindicated by his performance and still feeling his oats, Graham wasn't ready for the day to end. So, as the Giants were playing out the string in the top of the ninth, the Scranton star sent a batboy to the opposing dugout with a challenge to right fielder George Browne—the man he had replaced in his lone major league appearance. Browne fancied himself a speedy runner. During the short time Doc was with the Giants, the two had engaged in many discussions as to who was faster. Now, a race around the bases after the game could finally settle the dispute. Or not.

Although a group of Doc's friends in the stands took up a collection and gathered $50 to be given to the winner, Browne refused to race. He again declined the offer after his teammates learned of the challenge and contributed more money, raising the pot to $250. When the game ended and word began to circulate that the popular local wanted to race a member of McGraw's bad boys, a crowd gathered around the two players. More inducements were offered. The pot was raised to nearly $500, more than twice Graham's monthly salary. But Browne—one of the few Giants starters to play—wouldn't budge. It was then suggested that he come back the next day when he was a little more rested. "Sorry," Browne said. "I've got to be back in New York for a regular game." With that, he, McGraw, and the rest of the Giants marched over to the Lackawanna Railroad Depot, boarded their train, and steamed off into the gathering darkness.

As he stood on the platform and watched the train pull away, Graham must have realized that his dream of playing again for the Giants had ended. Left behind in Scranton, he played one more exhibition game—against the Baltimore Orioles of the Eastern League—and beat local sprint champion Al Reese in a footrace for $500, half of which he donated to the Scranton Consumptive Hospital. Then, as always, he unpacked his shingle and switched from playing to "practice." On September 24, the *Scranton Times* reported that "Dr. Graham will go abroad and spend the greater part of his time at a medical university in Germany in pursuit of his studies." But there is no evidence that actually happened. Instead, he returned to New York, where he continued his internship and for the first time since 1902 began thinking about life without baseball.

Yet even though medicine would start to become more of a priority while he cared for patients at Postgraduate, Lying-in, and Columbus hospitals during the next two years, Graham never let his dream of returning to the majors stop flickering. When the *Scranton Tribune* published a story stating that Graham might be traded or released by the Giants, he vehemently denied the rumor. "Graham says he is still retained by New York," the newspaper reported, "and that he has been assured by manager McGraw that he will continue on the Giants' roster next year."

As it turned out, Graham was fooling himself or McGraw went back on his word. Either way, Doc spent the next few seasons watching his major league rights bounce around among the Giants, the Boston Red Sox, and the Cleveland Indians. He would never come close to getting another sniff of a major league cup of coffee like the one he had enjoyed on June 29, 1905.

CHAPTER 5

Crossroads
Is There a Doctor in the House?

$\smile\!\!\!-$

*"There is no more popular player than
Graham on the team. Doc's departure from
the game will be regretted by the thousands
of fans in this city, with whom he is a prime
favorite and his success as a practitioner is
predicted."*

ITEM IN THE *SCRANTON TIMES,*
JUNE 13, 1907

IN HINDSIGHT, THE WINTER OF 1906–7 probably would have
been the perfect time for Doc Graham to leave baseball behind and begin concentrating on his medical career. He had
just led his team to a championship and won the New York
State League batting title, yet even his best season as a professional wasn't enough to keep him from getting released by the
Giants. With his medical degree in hand and an internship at
a prestigious big-city hospital, he was well on the way to making the transition from part-time ballplayer to full-time

doctor. He might actually have let it happen that off-season had the Boston Red Sox not purchased his contract and re-kindled his hope of getting back to the majors.

By the time he realized it wasn't going to happen, he had already committed to taking the summer off to play ball. So he went back to Scranton. It was the right choice, of course. As a ballplayer and a man, Graham was loved by people of the northeastern Pennsylvania town, and his return provided him a familiar and comfortable place to live and play. It also gave his fans renewed hope of another championship season.

But the chemistry just wasn't the same. Manager Eddie Ashenback had moved on to bigger and better things in Min-nesota with St. Paul of the American Association. In his place, the Miners hired Henry "Uncle Hank" Ramsey, a nice enough guy and a knowledgeable baseball man, but one who lacked his predecessor's knack for judging talent and relating to his players. Graham didn't like Ramsey right from the start, so he decided to hold out, figuring that if he had to play for the man, at least he could make a few extra dollars doing it. "Doc Graham has registered a kick on the salary proposition and refuses to play unless some more of the essential wherewithal is apportioned for his pay envelope," was the way the *Scranton Times* put it.

The standoff ended on the eve of the 1907 opener when the league's owners agreed to increase each team's salary lim-it by $150 a month, from $2,250 to $2,400. His raise secured, Graham reluctantly signed his contract, got on the train with star pitcher Bob Chappell—who had just been released by the Cincinnati Reds—and joined his team in Troy, New York. He walked and scored the season's first run in the top of the first in a 7–5 Scranton win, then went into hibernation. Or as the *Scranton Times* described it, "Doc Graham has failed so far to get his hitting clothes on. . . . We are anxiously awaiting the doctor." The wait would be a long one.

Graham went 0 for 2 in that first game, followed by 0 for 4 performances in the final two games of the series at Troy. He then came up empty in seven official at-bats in a 2–1 loss in 16 innings at Albany. In an effort to help him break out of his slump, Uncle Hank dropped his hitless doctor to third in the batting order, but that didn't help either.

When the Miners stumbled back to Scranton after their first road trip of the year, they were 2–3 with a tie, and their defending league batting champ was still wearing the weighty collar of a .000 average. Slow starts were nothing new to Graham. They were one of the occupational hazards of his moonlighting. Although he was finished with school, the young intern was spending more time than ever on his medical training.

Internships traditionally lasted only one year, but Graham had to divide his over two because of the time he missed playing baseball and because his required instruction was split among three different teaching hospitals. During the off-season of 1906–7, he did his general medical rotation at New York University's Postgraduate Hospital, now known as Tisch Hospital, located at First Avenue and 27th Street. The following year, he started his winter getting OB/GYN experience at Lying-in Hospital, a newly constructed eight-story facility at Second Avenue and 17th Street financed by millionaire J. Pierpont Morgan; that hospital is now known as Cornell University Medical Center. Graham completed his instruction at Columbia University Hospital on New York's Upper West Side. There, he prepared for his chosen specialties of optometry and ear, nose, and throat by doing extensive study of allergies and treatments for conditions involving the sinuses, the larynx, the thyroid, and the inner ear.

A typical day during his hospital internships called for a

full shift of caring for patients under a resident's supervision, then several more hours of lab work. He also spent many of his nights and weekends on call. Understanding the need to stay in shape, Graham tried to exercise whenever he could, which wasn't often, considering that he spent most days working from eight in the morning to eight at night. Although he occasionally found time for a quick jog, a few minutes of calisthenics, or even some tosses of a ball with another doctor, he had little or no chance to take batting practice against live pitching. That meant he had to hit his way back into form once he exchanged his lab coat for the knickers and cap of a ballplayer each spring.

While the fans and the local newspaper blamed his latest early-season struggle on his lack of preseason training, both Graham and team management were privately starting to worry. They hoped that the return to familiar surroundings and the excitement surrounding the Miners' home opener would provide the spark to jump-start his hitting. The celebration, held a day late because of rain, began with a parade that had the players and town officials marching around the courthouse square before boarding horse-drawn carriages for a procession to the ballpark. The bleachers were already filled to overflowing by the time they arrived about an hour before game time. At that point, Mayor J. B. Dimmick made his obligatory speech, threw out the first ball, and helped raise the 1906 pennant to the top of the Athletic Park flagpole. Then it was back to business as usual.

Graham almost broke his 0-for-the-season that chilly May day in a 5–0 win against Troy. In the fifth inning, he rocketed a line drive that seemed headed for the gap, but as the *Scranton Times* reported, "the hoodoo refused to leave his bat" when center fielder Rube DeGroff "made a circus catch of what was beyond a doubt a safe hit."

Doc Graham playing center field for the Scranton Miners in 1908, his final season as a professional baseball player
COURTESY OF THE *SCRANTON TIMES-TRIBUNE* ARCHIVES

The next day, May 18, in his 30th at-bat of the year, he finally got one to fall in for his first hit. He added another single in the bottom of the ninth and scored the winning run on a triple by shortstop Gus Ziemer.

The pressure now off, Graham was finally able to relax and go on the kind of tear that had become his trademark. He proved that the worst was over by banging out three more hits, including a homer, two games later against Albany. "Every indication is that Doc Graham will get his optic on the pill before long and will stride along with the .300-class swatsmiths," the *Times* predicted, even though his average was still a paltry .148. "Another week or so of warm weather and Doc will be in old-time form."

The problem was that the weather took a turn for the worse. A fierce cold snap, complete with snow showers, enveloped Upstate New York during the final week in May, bringing everything to a screeching halt and forcing the Miners to spend two idle days "warming their shins at the fireside in Utica" instead of playing. Conditions got so bad that several members of the team fell ill. Fortunately, they had brought a doctor along with them.

According to local news reports, Graham had his hands full administering to all the aches and pains. "It is reported that [George] Schultz burned his fingers on the pocket oil stove that he has been carrying and no more spitballs for him this season," the *Scranton Times* noted. "[Eddie] Shortell went out on the icy sidewalk and sprained his ankle. Hogan Yancey has the croup and has been wearing onion poultices. Gus Ziemer is suffering from the same affliction and Wilkie Clark is rubbing him with goose grease. McDougal, [Joe] Garrity and Rudinski are down with chills and [Perry] Polchow is threatening to go south. McArdle is drinking boiled apple-jack to keep his pipes open and Joe Schrall has chills so bad that his uniform won't stay on him. Johnny Duffy, who is a second cousin to the discoverer of the malt extract beverage, shivers and wishes he never left his own fireside. [Henry] Beckendorf is threatened with tonsillitis and worse than all, Ramsey has tabooed anything stronger than ginger ale and soda water. This is cruelty of the most aggravated kind and if the team ever gets out of the frigid zone, they will never forgive Ramsey."

As the season progressed and Ramsey's dictatorial style started to wear thin, the Miners did, in fact, come to despise their coach. For now, though, the players were much too cold and sick to worry about such trivial matters. If one positive came from that late-May snowstorm in Utica, it was that Doc Graham—a trained ear, nose, and throat specialist—was on hand to provide advice and care for his ailing teammates. Doing so reinforced the feeling that had been growing in his heart since the end of the previous season—that his desire to be a doctor was outgrowing his love for playing baseball.

When his team returned on June 12 from a road trip better suited for skiing than for pitching and hitting, Graham told management that he planned to retire at the end of the season. He then took a trip down to city hall to register with the local prothonotary as a practicing physician. Hanging his shingle was only a formality, of course. He'd been seeing patients in his spare time almost from the moment he passed the Pennsylvania state medical exam on January 2. Making it official only confirmed what everyone already assumed. Because of the mutual fondness he'd developed with the miners, factory workers, and railroad men who had supported him so well since he arrived, Graham planned to stay in Scranton and set up practice once his playing days were done.

In the meantime, he began to hit the baseball as though he had no plans to quit. On June 6, in a 4–3 loss to Utica, he went 4 for 4 in a performance the *Scranton Times* described as "the only redeeming feature" of the game. Graham, it said, "acted more like himself than at any time this season. . . . Four times up and as many times he was given credit for a swat." He followed that with nine more hits in his next five official games to raise his batting average to a much more Graham-like .249. In between, he got his final brush with major league greatness. Unfortunately, it wasn't his own.

More than a half-century later, in the movie *Field of Dreams*, the good doctor would play in a game with the great Shoeless Joe Jackson. In real life, on June 9, 1907, Doc Graham actually graced the same diamond as Hall of Famer Ty Cobb, considered by many as the greatest pure hitter of all time. On the day when Cobb and his Detroit Tigers stopped in Scranton to play an exhibition game, a rousing crowd of more than 8,000 jammed the grandstand, bleachers, and outfield grass at the Athletic Park. Cobb went 3 for 5 and scored two runs for the Tigers, who won 7–4.

Such contests were common in those days. Because radio was still in its infancy, few fans got the chance to hear live games involving the major leaguers they read about in the newspapers. So, on travel days, when their trains were scheduled to stop in minor league cities, big-league franchises would often get off and play local teams. The games were always eagerly anticipated by the fans. The owners loved them, too, because they provided a financial windfall for both teams, a few dollars being thrown in for the players to make it worth their while. On top of all that, the games gave the big-league organizations an opportunity to do some scouting for prospects. It wasn't uncommon for players to be signed to major league contracts on the spot after impressive performances.

By that time, though, Graham was no longer looking to make such an impression and prove he belonged with the big boys, as he had a year earlier against McGraw and the Giants. He went hitless in four official trips against the Tigers, though he did get hit by a pitch and drove in a run on a fielder's choice.

His resignation that he would never get back to the majors wasn't without its irony. Three days after Graham played against Cobb and the Tigers, the *Scranton Times* ran the story of his planned retirement at the end of the season. One column to the right, a prominent item out of New York, punctuated with a large illustration, reported, "After 14 years of active service upon the diamond, Manager McGraw of the New York Nationals declares he is tired of traveling and . . . may retire at the close of the present season, never to manage or play again." The fact that both would eventually change their minds and return in 1908 only linked them further among the baseball gods.

By the beginning of July, Graham raised his batting average to .256. As during the previous season, his inspired play became the catalyst for the entire team. Following a 19-inning 6–5 loss to Troy—in which Doc went 0 for 6—the Miners went on a tear that saw them rise from fifth to the top of the New York State League standings. They passed first-place Albany by a half-game on July 30 when Graham, now hitting second in the order, rapped out four hits in a 4–2 win against Utica.

His average rose to .278 and his team's lead in the standings grew to three games over Troy on August 16, when the Miners began a key stretch of eight games in two weeks against the second-place Trojans. When the teams split their home-and-home series straight down the middle, Scranton maintained its lead with a little less than three weeks remaining in the regular season. Dreams of a second straight championship began to take hold. "It will soon be time to change the numbers on the pennant at Athletic Park," the *Scranton*

Times predicted on August 24, the day after the Miners beat Albany 4–3 to extend their lead to four games.

Plans for a celebration, however, turned out to be premature. While Graham and his teammates did indeed leave Troy behind in the race for the 1907 title, they failed to see another team sneaking up behind them. That team was Albany, which won the final three games of its series in Scranton to jump right back into the race. Once they lost their momentum, the Miners were never able to get it back. They finished the season with an 81–54 record, two games behind the surging Senators.

The late-season collapse was a major disappointment to Graham, as was his .265 batting average, a 70-point drop-off from the season before. But take away that unsightly 0 for 29 start following his early-season holdout and his .303 average would actually have been the second-highest of his seven-year professional career. And as was the case in 1906, he saved his best hitting for the second half of the season, when his team needed it most.

Because of that production, Graham's quiet professionalism, and his popularity among the fans of Scranton, team president J. W. Barnes approached him within hours of the final game to ask him to reconsider his retirement. He declined at first, determined to begin his full-time medical practice. But by the turn of the new year, not long after it was announced that manager Ramsey would not be retained, he gave in to the pressure and agreed to come back for one more season. Barnes announced the news in the *Scranton Times* on January 2, 1908, in a story denying a report that either Graham or Joe Schrall would be traded to Binghamton for outfielder Lew McAllister.

As it turned out, Schrall *was* dealt away—to Syracuse, not Binghamton—when the league's owners got together for their annual winter meetings three weeks later. Graham, on the other hand, wasn't going anywhere. He was much too valuable to the Miners. Besides, if he had been sent to another team, he would simply have retired again, rather than leave Scranton.

Now that Graham's spot on the team was all but guaranteed, his biggest concern that winter was who Barnes would hire to manage the team. Graham publicly lobbied for Eddie Ashenback. It would have been a good choice had Ashenback not already signed to manage Johnstown in the outlaw Tri-State League. Instead, Barnes opted for Malachi Kittredge, a former catcher for the Chicago Cubs.

Although Kittredge had major league managerial experience, it wasn't anything to brag about. In 1904, he had lasted 17 games with the hapless Washington Senators, winning only once, before being replaced by Patsy Donovan. But he did get at least one thing out of the brief experience—contacts, and plenty of them. They paid off royally when Kittredge got to Scranton and was handed a roster with only three returning players—Graham, shortstop Gus Ziemer, and young Henry Beckendorf, who had taken over as the starting catcher late the previous season, after Wilkie Clark was suspended for throwing a bat into the stands in Wilkes-Barre.

Calling in favors from everyone he knew, Kittredge brought in pitcher Elmer Steele from the Red Sox, second baseman Charley Moran from the Senators, and pitcher Joseph Bills from Connie Mack's Philadelphia Athletics. He acquired first baseman Ben Houser from Rochester of the Eastern League and rescued third baseman Mike Madigan off the scrap heap. He recruited pitcher Howard Mittinger off the campus of Penn State and stole Frank Eley and James Robertson from archrival Wilkes-Barre. A practicing dentist from Fordham University, Robertson joined Graham to give the Miners the best and most extensive medical staff in the league.

The team's lineup wasn't bad either. With Graham back in the leadoff spot, the Kitties—as the local newspaper started calling the team in honor of its new manager—followed a similar pattern to the one that had worked so well for them in their championship season of 1906. They got off to a fast start before settling comfortably into second place, a few games behind Binghamton. Then they made their move in early June when the league-leading Bingoes came to town for the first time. After a four-game sweep that leapfrogged them to the top of the standings, they stayed there for virtually the rest of the season. But it wasn't nearly as easy as it sounds.

First, there was Graham, who got off to his now-customary slow start. Then came an epidemic of injuries and defections that forced Kittredge to do more juggling than a circus sideshow performer. It started when Madigan, the opening-day right fielder, was hit in the head with a batted ball and missed more than a month. He was replaced by Eley, who soon shifted over to center when Jocko Halligan decided to leave the team for no apparent reason. Robertson then became the regular right fielder, but because the bench was so thin, pitchers Bills and Mittinger were often asked to fill in as outfielders. The situation didn't improve when Madigan returned. Within days, he was asked to move to third base when Heine Groh broke his arm and was lost for the season. At various times during the summer, Eley and Houser, a big left-hander who developed into one of the best hitters in the league, were also disabled. Steele was recalled by the Red Sox. And yet, as the *Scranton Times* noted, "accidents did not cut any figure in the standing of the team."

But one accident in early August threatened to literally send Scranton's championship season up in flames. A fire engulfed the Athletic Park, leaving the main grandstand a smoldering heap of charred lumber. The disaster left the team homeless, at least temporarily, and forced owner E. J. Coleman to reschedule a number of games for the road. Distracted by the events back home, the Miners lost six of the eight games on their extended, unscheduled trip to Elmira—where the A.J. & G. Jags had relocated—and Binghamton to briefly fall into second place.

They eventually got over the shock and righted the ship. As usual, the catalyst for the hot streak was Dr. Archibald Graham. Batting around .250 at the time, Graham geared up for his annual big finish by collecting three hits in a double-header sweep of Syracuse that helped his team regain the league lead. From there, Scranton went to Binghamton for a regularly scheduled three-game series. Graham again got his team off to a fast start by going 3 for 5 with a homer and three runs scored in a 10–3 victory. Two more wins against the Bingoes followed, giving the Miners a four-game lead and a 75–44 record when they made their triumphant and long-awaited return home on September 8. Albany didn't stand a chance. "Amid the ruins of the grandstand at Athletic Park," the *Scranton Times* reported, "the Kitties went after the [defending] champions and ran them off their feet, taking the game by the score of 4–0." Graham did his part in the game that all but wrapped up Scranton's second pennant in three years by amassing three hits and scoring three of the four runs. The official clincher came on September 12, an occasion made even sweeter by the fact that it came against the hated Barons of Wilkes-Barre.

Although Graham went 0 for 5 in his final regular-season game, his September surge catapulted his season average nearly 30 points, to .277, and his 75 runs were a career high.

Retirement awaited, for real this time, but the good doctor still had a little bit of baseball left in him, thanks to a

Class B "championship series" against Tri-State League winner Williamsport. The best-of-three showdown, to be played at the home stadium of Connie Mack's Philadelphia Athletics, was arranged by George M. Graham, the longtime sports editor of the *Philadelphia North American*.

While the details were being worked out, the Miners played a pair of exhibition games against a group of local amateurs to stay sharp. The series against Williamsport was finally scheduled by September 26. By that time, Ziemer and Mittinger had already left town. Pitcher Al Kellogg was also unavailable after being recalled by the Athletics. It didn't matter. Already well schooled in the art of overcoming adversity, what was left of Kittredge's team easily won the first two games to finish the season in triumph. In his final hurrah as a professional baseball player, Graham contributed a hit and a run in a 5–3 Scranton win. Immediately after the game, the veteran leftfielder and all but three other members of the team were placed on the reserve list to protect them for 1909. But this time, there was no convincing Graham to come back. In what proved to be his professional epitaph, the *Scranton News* wrote, "This fair city of ours has had many esteemed ball tossers, but none that can surpass the high standard set by the medical athlete."

Four years earlier, he had arrived in northeastern Pennsylvania as a disappointed young ballplayer with designs on staying only long enough to earn his way back to the major leagues. Over time, he evolved into a confident, mature doctor who thought he'd found a place to plant some roots. He fell in love with Scranton because, like Doc Graham himself, it was a contradiction of considerable proportions. Framed by the lush green peaks of the Pocono Mountains, which rolled on as far as the eye could see, the area was a bustling, booming tribute to the industrial revolution. Known as a railroad hub and coal-mining center, Scranton at the turn of the 20th century was a maze of foundries, furnaces, and manufacturing works, not to mention the home of the largest stationary engine in the United States. For the most part, its people were honest, unpretentious blue-collar laborers, many of them immigrants, who understood the meaning of a hard day's work. They were the kind of people to whom Graham related best, which was why he thought so seriously about staying among them once his baseball-playing days were over.

In many ways, the four years Graham spent in Scranton were the best and most memorable of his life, at least athletically. It was a time he never forgot. In addition to returning frequently to visit and to attend games at the newly rebuilt Minooka Park, he commemorated the good old days by sending gifts to the sports editor of the local newspaper every year around Christmas. "He was the most appreciative ballplayer that the *News* ever came into contact with and was an incalculable credit to the game," the *Scranton News* wrote during the 1940s. "Every little act or favor or consideration that the sporting writers used to do for Doc was safely tucked back into some secluded nook in his memory and he never forgot it. Just to show that he had no hard feelings and that his thoughts once in a while turn back to the city where he spent his baseball days—as he himself says—he ships on a Merry Xmas box of the choicest Havana fillers that can be found this side of Cuba."

Graham never really wanted to leave Scranton. He probably would have settled there and become part of the community had it not been for the persistent cough and chronic tightness he developed in his lungs, most likely from the smoke and other residue that poured daily from the massive furnace stacks that dominated the city's skyline. As much as he didn't want to, the doctor in him knew he had to leave. So when he received an offer of a residency at the Chicago Eye and Ear Hospital, he packed his shingle, his medical bag, and all his other worldly possessions and moved on to begin the next phase of his life.

CHAPTER 6

Northern Exposure
"I Am Here. I Am Your Doctor."

―――――

*"Following his internship in the great hospitals
and medical centers of the east, this healer of men
could have commanded the highest paid positions
in the largest and most advanced hospitals. Instead, he chose to come to a new, growing community of lumberjacks, miners and toiling farmers."*
EDITORIAL IN THE *CHILSHOLM TRIBUNE-
PRESS*, AUGUST 31, 1965

FOLKS FROM THE IRON RANGE of northern Minnesota know it
as "the call of the Mesabi." But it's not something that can be
heard, like the dynamite blasts that still occasionally resound
from the old Hull Rust Mine a few miles away in Hibbing. It's
more of a feeling, an attraction that inexplicably bonds people
with the land the way a magnet would be drawn to the rich
vein of iron ore beneath the region's rolling hills. So strong is

the lure of "the Sleeping Giant," as the Ojibwa Indians referred
to it, that it becomes part of a man's soul once he's heeded its
call.

It happened to Archie Graham on April Fool's Day in
1909.

No one is quite sure why the young doctor—Carolina-
born, Johns Hopkins–educated, and New York–trained—
traveled halfway across the country to set up his first practice.
Or why he chose to stay in a corner of the Minnesota wild so
remote a later acquaintance described it as "the kind of place
people can't wait to leave." But he did.

Graham was in Rochester, Minnesota, attending a medical conference at the Mayo Clinic when he first heard about
Chisholm and the Iron Range. They were mentioned to him
by a colleague when Graham complained that the persistent cough he'd developed while playing ball in Scranton just
wouldn't seem to go away. When the conference ended, the
friend suggested that Graham go up to the range where "the
air is pure and they have the best water on earth."

The same could have been said of any number of places,
including the mountain city of Asheville, North Carolina, a
well-known destination for lung patients. But after spending
seven years playing ball and studying in places such as New
York, Baltimore, Chicago, and Pennsylvania, Graham had
become increasingly detached from most of his family. He
remained close only to older brother David, a Marine Corps
member stationed in Puerto Rico at the time, and younger
brother Frank, still a student at UNC. The prospect of returning home, therefore, no longer appealed to him. Neither did
the lengthy cross-country trek required to get him there.

Since he was already in Minnesota, Graham chose to heed
the advice of his friend. Instead of going back to the Chicago
Eye and Ear Hospital, where he'd worked as a resident the pre-

vious six months, he wired in his resignation and left civilization as he knew it. Armed with a 1908 medical journal that contained a Help Wanted ad seeking a doctor for the Mesabi Clinic's district office in St. Louis County, he went to the railroad station and told the clerk for the Great Northern Railroad to give him a ticket "for as far north as the train goes."

The tracks ended in Chisholm.

Graham's first inclination upon his arrival was to get right back onto the train and head somewhere else. It was brutally cold. A dusting of snow covered the ground. A wintry wind whipped up a healthy chop on nearby Longyear Lake. What he saw around him was even less inspiring. Everywhere were the charred remains of a city almost completely destroyed by a devastating wildfire the previous fall. What hadn't been reduced to ash or scarred by fire was covered by the gritty, reddish brown ore residue stirred up by the digging at the region's 15 working mines.

Across the tracks from the platform, workers scurried busily around the yard at King Lumber Company preparing and delivering supplies to workers rebuilding the downtown area. It had been almost seven months since the blaze that began in a logging camp northwest of town and spread rapidly with a shifting wind. The smell of burned wood and ash remained heavy in the air. Rubble littered the streets. A few blocks from the train depot on the city's main drag, Lake Street, only the school and the Catholic church had escaped complete destruction.

Not that Chisholm had been much to look at before the fire. Founded eight years earlier by Duluth developer Archibald Chisholm because of its real-estate potential in proximity to the many surrounding mines, the town looked like something out of a Western movie. Among the early structures were a bank, a general store, and, of course, at least two

View of downtown Chisholm from the top of Lake Street after the fire
COURTESY OF THE CITY OF CHISHOLM, MINNESOTA

or three saloons. Tents and temporary two-room wooden shacks built for about $300 per structure stood along a central avenue that was, according to residents, "a fairly good trail through stumps, through which any good teamster could drive."

Although the cleanup and restoration effort of 1909 was well under way by the time Graham arrived, Chisholm was still in a shambles. Many of those displaced by the fire had moved to nearby Hibbing. Those who had returned were living in temporary hovels and other makeshift structures. Most people had lost everything they owned, prompting members of the fire department to set up circus tents at the Central School to distribute food and clothing. Even the most affluent members of the community looked and lived as though they were vagrants.

As depressing as the scene was, Graham found himself intrigued by the spirit of the townspeople working so hard to pick up the pieces and put the disaster behind them. Besides, he wasn't thrilled about the prospect of another long trip in a cramped coach car. So he decided to stay awhile. He asked for directions, walked down Central Avenue, took a left on Lake Street toward the Rood Hospital on the corner of Second Avenue Southwest and Fifth Street, and knocked on the door. When nurse K. A. Murray opened it to see who was there, Graham introduced himself. "I am here. I am your doctor," he said.

Although the job and the surroundings were unlike anything he'd ever experienced, Graham adjusted quickly. It was a match almost as contradictory as the young doctor himself. Despite his more urban upbringing and training, the young doctor found that he enjoyed the solitude of small-town living. He took long, introspective walks across town early every morning. Professionally, the slower pace and lack of pretentiousness among his colleagues allowed him to be himself and helped him fit in better than he ever had at any of those big-city hospitals back east. Most of all, he admired the hardworking miners under his care. "In a region so intent upon scooping wealth from raw material, it neglected to look after its human raw material," he observed years later.

The well-bred, well-educated doctor developed an unexpected bond with the local men, most of them recent immigrants from Croatia, Serbia, Germany, and Scandinavia who spoke little or no English. He built lasting relationships with them based on trust and mutual respect. He often went above and beyond the call of duty to try to make their lives a little more bearable. Graham organized night-school classes that helped the men and their families prepare to become citizens. He made after-hours house calls whenever summoned and sat up all night with sick children. He was especially attentive to expectant mothers, often getting out of bed in the middle of the night to help them deliver their babies. "Every doctor knows that women undergo a situation more desperate than machine gun fire; yet they do not whimper but face the inevitable," he said. "I for one would like to see a monument, made of the most beautiful marble and higher than the Empire State Building, erected to the 'unknown mother.' Not the mother here or there, but the mother everywhere . . . this mother holding a new-born babe." In the eight years Graham worked at the Rood Hospital, Chisholm averaged about 30 births a month. The hospital's standard charge was $5 per delivery. Twins cost $7.50, and triplets were $10.

As much work as he did for the mothers and others in Chisholm, he rarely, if ever, asked to be compensated for his services, other than requesting an occasional place at the dinner table with the family for a home-cooked meal. Sometimes on his way home from their impoverished but tight-knit neighborhood—known as Pig Town for the livestock that roamed its streets—Graham would stop by the local ball field, lean against the fence, and watch the young men play. It wasn't long before he began to feel the old itch again. Eventually, he stopped watching and began joining in the games. Despite being out of shape, and suffering the lingering effects of a respiratory problem he would later swear was tuberculosis, Graham still had his skills. He never told his new friends about his one game with the Giants, saying only that he'd "played a little minor league ball."

When word of the baseball-playing doctor reached Brin Freeman, the captain of Chisholm's entry in the semipro Mesaba Range League, he wasted little time recruiting Graham to play for the team. Graham first balked at the offer, telling Freeman that he needed to concentrate on his duties at the hospital. But shortly after the season began on June 19, he changed his mind and agreed to play when it didn't interfere with his work schedule.

Graham, now known as "Doc" rather than "Moonlight," made his debut on July 22 against the Biwabik Miners. Not surprisingly, he had an immediate impact. On the first strike he saw, he connected on a screaming line drive that sent "the right fielder running a mile," according to a newspaper account. Although the ball was caught, teammate Bill Vogts tagged up from third and scored the first run of a 3–1 Chisholm victory. As he returned to the dugout to the congratulations of his new teammates, it was as if Graham had been reborn. Nothing was more intoxicating to him than the feeling of making solid contact and the sound of fans cheering for him. He couldn't wait to experience it again.

It was just like old times, only now instead of playing ball first and being a doctor in his spare time, the opposite was true for Graham. He played mostly on Thursdays and Sundays, performing so well that by early August the *Chisholm Herald* praised him with a familiar description: "Graham was in left field and . . . is so fast on his feet he burns up the ground under him. When it comes to the stick, he makes all those pitchers look like monkeys."

At that point, Graham hadn't decided whether he wanted to stay in Chisholm or get out before winter arrived and the weather turned bad. His success on the baseball field helped convince him to stick around. So did the rapid rebuilding effort going on around him. All through town, modern brick buildings were sprouting up as rapidly as the buckwheat crop native to the area. Among the new developments was a baseball stadium, complete with electric lights for night games, a 500-seat grandstand, and bleachers that could hold another 300 fans.

Down at the other end of Lake Street, the new Rood Hospital was even more impressive. Described by the local newspaper as "first class in every particular," the two-story facility was paid for by a coalition of area mine owners, who wanted to keep their employees healthy to ensure that the stream of rich iron ore would continue uninterrupted. The hospital featured running hot water and a varnished Georgia pine finish throughout the patient area. The first floor consisted of a private office for Dr. A. B. Kirk, the physician in charge, and a sleeping room for the doctor on call overnight. It also included an operating room filled with the most modern equipment available, an emergency room, a dressing room for less serious cases, and a fully stocked dispensary. Upstairs on the second floor was a residence for Dr. Kirk, finished with the "richest birch obtainable." Two ambulances were stationed at the nearby Shenango Mine. Another, drawn by two horses, was kept at the hospital.

The new medical facility proved a godsend the following summer when a typhoid epidemic swept through northern

Minnesota and hit the Iron Range hard. A constant state of emergency gripped the town in August and September 1910. Known as "the Flying Death," typhoid fever is a bacterial disease spread by the common housefly and contracted by ingesting contaminated food or water. The residents of Chisholm had gotten their first hint of it a year earlier when poor sanitation and an abundance of standing water from the previous year's firefighting effort led to an increased fly population. "There were three large dairies in the middle of the residential district," Graham said years later in a newspaper interview. "Flies were so thick that if you ate a piece of pie in some of the restaurants, you had to bite twice to tell which you were eating, blueberries or flies."

Because conditions hadn't improved and the chlorination of the city's water system was still more than a year away, the local newspaper ran a story on May 31, 1910, warning people to take precautions. Among the suggestions: Don't allow flies in your house; don't permit them near your food, especially milk; don't buy foodstuffs where flies are tolerated; don't let flies swarm upon the nipple of a baby's bottle. Chisholmites were urged to clean their houses inside and out and to be careful to dispose of materials such as horse manure and "kitchen offal" in the proper manner. Graham tried to do his part to alert the public by urging his friends and everyone else he met to install screens on their windows and doors. He also campaigned for the clearing of infested swamps. Unfortunately, not everyone heeded the warnings.

Two months after the *Chisholm Tribune* told readers that "flies kill a greater number of human beings than all the beasts of prey, with all the poisonous serpents added," its words became tragically prophetic. The trouble began in early August, when the newspaper reported that Chisholm was "in the clutches of a dreaded epidemic" described as acute dysentery attributed to flies. Within a week, the disease led to 14 deaths, with "new cases being found every day." The outbreak, officially classified as typhoid by the Minnesota Board of Health on August 29, kept Graham and his colleagues working night and day. Many times, Graham didn't even bother leaving the hospital, opting instead to catch a few hours of sleep on a spare bed or a waiting-room couch. His efforts helped saved countless infected patients. But not everyone was so lucky. When all was said and done, the typhoid plague had claimed nearly 100 victims in Chisholm and nearby Hibbing.

The epidemic also put an end to any opportunity Graham might have had to earn his way back to organized baseball. Thanks to Jack Sheridan, designated by American League president Ban Johnson as both chief umpire and talent scout, Doc's contract became the property of the Boston Red Sox as the typhoid fly was wreaking havoc on the youth of Chisholm. Sheridan had already come across several prospects during his travels to Minnesota that summer. Eddie Korger, a youngster from St. Paul also picked up by Boston, was considered a find. Hibbing's star pitcher, Jack Gilligan, ended up with Toledo of the American Association.

Like the fans who witnessed the Mesaba Range League games in 1909 and 1910, Sheridan was impressed by Graham's diamond skills, even though he displayed them only sporadically because of his medical obligations. After watching a few games and learning that the town doctor had once played for McGraw's Giants, Sheridan concluded that there was still a possibility that the speedy, strong-armed outfielder could resume professional play. Because of his extensive experience in pro ball, his thin frame, and his commendable dietary habits, Graham seemed an excellent bet to return to top form easily and quickly. Thus, Sheridan offered him a contract, assuming that with the benefit of a rigorous spring training to help get him back in shape, he could assist the Red Sox in 1911, probably as a reserve.

How Graham reacted to that offer is not difficult to envision. Probably flattered and tempted momentarily, he wasn't naive enough to believe that major league playing time beckoned him at the age of 31. He had come to be the city's doctor at a time of disease and distress, and he was not about to break his pledge. He recognized that he was needed, especially by the area's youth, and that need—not the lure of a boyhood fantasy—topped his list of priorities. By 1910, he recognized that he played baseball for fun and practiced medicine for keeps.

The citizens of Chisholm probably knew nothing of Sheridan's offer. No record exists that Graham ever discussed it with anyone—not in 1910, not ever. Quietly and compassionately, he continued with his medical practice.

But that didn't mean baseball was out of his system. He continued to play for the city team and in local industrial leagues until he was almost 50. And during his many travels to Rochester and back east, he never passed up the opportunity to go to the old ball yard and take in a game. One such excursion back to Scranton, Pennsylvania, during the summer of 1911 was chronicled by the *Chisholm Tribune-Herald* under the headline, "Dr. Graham Was a Ball Player."

"When he left Chisholm two weeks ago for his annual vacation, he went back to his old stomping grounds at Scranton and the very first day found him in the stands where he could observe the antics of the present day Scranton team," the article read. Although the *Tribune-Herald* noted that Graham was "always calm and reserved," acting more like "the son of a Methodist minister" or a "student of theology" than a raucous ballplayer, his old instincts came out upon his return to Minooka Park. Wearing a straw hat and sitting in the grandstand behind home plate for a game against Albany, Graham watched as a Scranton player named O'Hara tripled, then stood on third base trying to catch his breath. "That man needs an anesthetic," Doc called out to anyone who would listen.

When outfielder Chick Hartley made a running one-handed catch, the kind Graham was noted for in his playing days, Doc shouted, "Ought to amputate that left arm, for sure." Ironically, just like his new admirer in the stands, Hartley boasted a major league career that had consisted of just one game with the New York Giants. At least he had gotten four at-bats in his game, on June 4, 1902. Although he went hitless, he did walk, steal a base, and make two putouts in left field.

Graham stayed in Scranton for three or four days, making a short side trip to neighboring Wilkes-Barre to see old friend and skipper Eddie Ashenback, whose Syracuse team was in town to play the local nine. Then he hopped on a train and headed for New York to renew acquaintances with friends from his days as a med student, to watch his old Giants play, and perhaps to daydream for a moment or two of what might have been.

"Although the doctor weakly intimates that he has no longing to return to the game, when he crosses his legs and sort of catches his breath, he announces that the side should have been retired," the *Scranton Daily Republican* reported on June 16, 1911. "A man on third with only one out plays on Graham's nerves just as he used to do, for there are delicate jobs with the surgeon's knife, but there is no job so delicate as removing a run from the man on third. Since his base ball days he has taken on an M.D. look, but still enjoys the crack of the bat and the story of Casey's downfall."

As Chisholm continued to grow and prosper, so did Doc

Graham. By 1910, the town's population swelled to a robust 7,684. Within another year, most reminders of the great fire were long gone. Now firmly embedded in the community, Graham decided it was time to begin putting down some roots. In June 1911, he was nominated by his boss, Dr. Kirk, and a friend, J. H. McNiven, for membership in the local Masonic lodge, one of several fraternal and civic organizations he would join.

It was about that same time when Graham first ran into Chisholm school superintendent James P. Vaughan on the way home from one of his frequent house calls to Pig Town. Vaughan, three years Graham's junior, was already an important figure in town, having answered "the call of the Mesabi" shortly after arriving in 1907. He was so well respected that after the fire, he was one of a handful of prominent leaders chosen to be on a committee overseeing the rebuilding effort. Under Vaughan's leadership—and with a major assist from the local mines that pumped unheard-of amounts of money into the building of facilities and the hiring of staff—Chisholm's schools were among the best in the nation. A reporter from the *Chicago Herald,* sent to Minnesota in 1916 to investigate charges of extravagance on the part of Iron Range school systems, concluded that Vaughan's "work and spirit . . . [are] the finest I have ever seen and . . . [are] not dependent on money."

Of course, the money didn't hurt. In 1915, it helped pay for a new high school that included a domestic sciences facility, a print shop, a gymnasium, an assembly hall, and laboratories, among other amenities, including Vaughan's office. The money also allowed for competitive salaries that gave the aggressive superintendent the freedom to recruit a much more talented faculty than could be expected for such an out-of-the-way location. Vaughan made so much money himself that when he was courted by the University of Wisconsin to become its president during the Depression, he turned the job down because its salary was considerably less than the $7,500 per year he was making in Chisholm.

Though they came from different areas of the country and had different interests, Graham and Vaughan were amazingly similar in many respects. Both grew up in families of nine children in which education was a valued commodity. Both went to college, then left home to pursue graduate degrees and become doctors. A Phi Beta Kappa member, Vaughan had earned his Ph.D. in philosophy at Wisconsin. While Graham was interested in the sciences, particularly medicine, Vaughan gravitated toward the humanities. His book, *Educational Democracy*, was considered well ahead of its time. With the help of his future wife, elementary-school teacher Leathe Wright, he developed a curriculum that was copied by school systems throughout the Midwest for years to come.

Like Graham, Vaughan would go on to become known as a mentor, leader, and visionary who was respected and loved throughout the community. But in those early days when they first met and became friends, they were simply two strong-willed men who enjoyed reading, dreaming up and testing new theories, and engaging in intelligent conversation—something that wasn't always easy to find among the uneducated miners with whom they lived. As their friendship grew, they became inseparable.

Vaughan, a farm boy at heart and by upbringing, chose to live in Pig Town because it allowed him to be closer to those he was hired to serve. He soon convinced his friend to do the same, though on his doctor's salary, Graham could easily have lived up on the hill with the more affluent members of society. "Of all places, [Doc] came to a mining town, where he took care of the old immigrants," another friend observed years later. "And the old immigrant population in this area, they were certainly needy. Many of them couldn't speak English, and yet [Graham] and J. P. Vaughan were the two individuals who were absorbed by that part of the community."

When Graham played ball, Vaughan would often come down to the park to watch. Other times, Graham would walk over to the high school, hang out in Vaughan's office, and spend hours listening to his friend espouse his opinions on the value of scholarship. The superintendent believed that a sound education strengthened the moral consciousness and tempered the soul. He took great pleasure in "awakening the creative joy" in his pupils and playing a role in steering them onto the path for a successful life.

Anxious to share his friend's vision and passion, Graham suggested that the local school system could use a staff physician. Vaughan agreed. Thanks to his nearly unlimited budget, funded almost entirely by the local mining companies, he created the position. On July 1, 1917, he hired Dr. A. W. Graham of the Rood Hospital to fill it. Another "call" had been answered.

CHAPTER 7

Miss Flower
The Doctor Takes a Wife

———

"His wife was a beautiful woman, a good woman. Very nice, very quiet. She was always in the background. She was not only attractive, she was a beautiful person. She always let Doc do his thing."

CHISHOLM BARBER FRANK TANCABEL

SHE WAS SO BEAUTIFUL AND DAINTY that the children in her class liked to call her "Miss Flower." Alecia Vicentia Madden had that kind of effect on people. So it came as no surprise that within months of her arrival in Chisholm in 1912, the pretty new schoolteacher with the cheery disposition and ever-present smile caught the eye of a certain country doctor.

Doc Graham was hardly the only eligible bachelor in town with designs on courting the popular Miss Flower. But because of his friendship with school superintendent J. P. Vaughan, Alecia's first cousin from back home in Rochester,

Alecia Graham, known to her students as "Miss Flower," was a dainty woman admired by nearly everyone she met—especially a certain Chisholm doctor.
COURTESY OF THE LYNN WILLIAMSON DIDIER COLLECTION

he had an advantage that at least got him in the door.

The fact that the two ended up together is a testament to the theory that opposites attract. Other than their large families and the respiratory problems that helped lead them to the fresh, pure air of the Iron Range, Doc and Alecia had little in common. He was a nonpracticing Presbyterian born into a family of pure-blooded Scottish Highlanders. She was a second-generation Irish Catholic whose family left Ireland during the potato famine of 1850 to claim farmland in the Wisconsin Territory and later, when it opened, Minnesota. He was outgoing and worldly, while she was an understated homebody. He was from a city in the South, while she grew up on a farm in the Midwest. He was also six years her senior.

Maybe that explained why the popular doctor and the pretty young teacher chose to conceal their relationship from all but their closest friends. Privately, their love was in full bloom by the time Graham traveled to Rochester to have his chronic breathing difficulties evaluated in early 1915. He spent several weeks at the Mayo Clinic and wrote to Alecia frequently. It was a frustrating period, not only because the doctors there were unable to find the cause of his ailment but also because of the time he had to spend away from his devoted fiancée. In one of his letters from the solitude of his room at the Hotel Zumbro, he expressed his feelings: "I am thinking of you all the time and wishing I could XXX you." A few weeks later, after dating quietly for nearly three years, they surprised everyone by announcing their engagement.

The wedding was held on September 15 at St. John's Church in Rochester. It was a grand affair on a picture-perfect Saturday morning, the bride looking angelic in her gown of white Georgette crepe with satin, ornamented with pearl trimmings and a traditional veil. Among those in the wedding party were her parents, Martin and Mary Madden; a cousin from Austin,

Minnesota, Miss Margaret Cotter; and Alecia's sisters, Mae, Genevieve, Grace, and Josephine. Although the service went off without a hitch, it wasn't without its uneasy moments. Because Doc wasn't Catholic and had no intention of converting, Father Murphy, the charismatic but hot-blooded priest at St. John's, refused to marry the couple in the main sanctuary in front of the altar of God. His unwillingness to budge caused considerable anguish among the wedding party, especially the bride, until a compromise was reached and it was decided that the vows would be exchanged next door in the rectory.

Following the nuptials, the wedding party and about 50 guests headed out to the Madden family farm for a festive reception. Known as Silver Creek, the farm was located about nine miles to the east in Viola. It was a sprawling compound with cows, pigs, and other livestock grazing on one side and rows of corn growing as far as the eye could see on the other. Overlooking it all atop a small, grassy bluff was a neat two-story house with a large covered porch that, according to the local newspaper, was adorned for the occasion in "a happy scheme of pink and white with suggestions of the autumn season."

About the only thing missing from the affair was Graham's family. Archie's beloved older brother, David, couldn't make it because his Marine Corps unit was stationed in Hawaii. The fact that no one else, especially his parents, made the trip to Minnesota for the happy day fueled speculation that the folks back home did not endorse his marriage to a Catholic girl. While it's true that Alexander and Kate Graham, both strong-willed Presbyterians, weren't thrilled about the situation, their absence had more to do with the difficulty of cross-country travel than with their religious beliefs. In fact, before honeymooning in New York, the doctor and his bride took a side trip to North Carolina so Alecia could meet the clan.

J.H. KAHLER, PRES. & MANAGING DIRECTOR.

Hotel Zumbro
THE ZUMBRO HOTEL CO. PROPS.

Rochester, Minn.

Dear Alicia:

The doctors here have examined me and are unable to find any ailment. There are so many new stunts here that it behooved me to embibe a few.

The rates to California are not on until Sunday so I still have time for absorption.

Met a girl — a nurse — cousin of Mamie Fawler. Met another girl in laboratory. When she

The letter Archie sent to Alecia while he was in Rochester just before their wedding in 1915
COURTESY OF THE LYNN WILLIAMSON DIDIER COLLECTION

learned that I was from the Range, she said she had my number.

There is a doctor here from my home town. We used to sell papers when we were a couple of kids.

He is Dr. Beckman's first asst., and has been here two years. His name is Irwin.

There is a building near the clinic building that looks like house on postal. There is a school house between this house & clinic. Am I right?

I am thinking of you all the time & wishing I could XXX you

archie

Once they returned home, the newlywed couple began settling into their life together in Chisholm.

Alecia was a beautiful woman barely five feet tall. She had peaches-and-cream skin, alluring powder-blue eyes, and long, dark, wavy brown hair that she usually wore in a bun. About her only physical flaw was the thick "piano" legs the other girls at school teased her about, usually behind her back. She had far too much confidence in herself to let petty jealousy and insults bother her, though. She was also a bright and adventurous woman who, like her seven brothers and sisters, was encouraged to pursue opportunities outside the boundaries of the family farm. Her brother Leo became a successful pharmacist in St. Paul. Another brother, Walter, earned fame as a champion golfer, went to law school, and received an appointment on the South Dakota Insurance Commission. Sisters Mae, Grace, and Josephine all acquired their teaching degrees, while Genevieve—known to her family as "Jen"—opened a needlework store, My Lady's Shop, on Rochester's main street, Broadway.

Alecia graduated from the Winona Seminary in 1906 at the age of 20. Two years later, she received her bachelor's degree in education from the University of Minnesota in Minneapolis. Rather than go right to work in the classroom, Alecia let her adventurous side get the best of her. She and her sister Jen began talking about an opportunity to spend some time in the wilds of the South Dakota plains. The Kincaid Act provided homesteaders up to 320 acres of land if they agreed to live on it for a full year. That wasn't easy, given the frontier conditions and harsh winters. But the Madden sisters—like thousands of other women seeking investments to pay off their education or support themselves and their families—took Uncle Sam up on the offer and staked a claim. Alecia left for Capa, South Dakota, on June 26, 1908. Except for a trip home for Christmas, she and Jen remained there until they fulfilled the terms of their claim. Shortly thereafter, they sold the land for a healthy profit and divided the money among themselves, their parents, and their grateful siblings.

Upon returning from her year on the prairie, Alecia began her teaching career in the Twin Cities. She also flirted with the idea of becoming an actress. In February 1911, she starred as the female lead in *Trelawney of the Wells*, a Sir Arthur Wing Pinero production centered around the theme that you can take the girl out of the country, but you can't take the country out of the girl. Alecia's performance got a rave review from the *Minneapolis Journal*. Her theatric aspirations soon became an afterthought, however, when her chronic hay fever began acting up about a year later, prompting her move north to Chisholm to pursue her true calling.

About the only thing she loved more than teaching was the children she taught. But because prevailing attitudes of the era frowned upon married women holding jobs, Alecia left the school system to become a homemaker shortly after marrying her doctor and becoming Mrs. Graham. It was a new role that took some growing into. Cooking was a particular challenge, as illustrated by the entries in her handwritten recipe book. Although she enjoyed baking and had a few sophisticated entries, such as chocolate spice cake, most of the recipes were far more basic. Among them: boiled macaroni.

If Archie was bothered by his new wife's lack of domestic skills, he never showed it or complained about it. During the day, while he was busy at his office in the Washington School, Alecia would often drop by to work with the children as an unofficial drama instructor and director for the school's many plays and pageants. In the afternoons when he made his usual house calls, he would always stick around with his patients long enough for dinner. He never forgot Alecia, though. Before leaving dinner, he would make sure to get a package—complete with ethnic treats such as homemade raised donuts and walnut pechska—so she could eat well, too. After dinner, they would retire to the parlor to spend the evening together reading and talking. She always called him "Docky," never Archie, A. W., or anything else. He called her "Deary" or "Honey."

About a year after they were married, the Grahams received an unexpected house guest when Doc's younger brother Frank came from New York to visit. It wasn't entirely a social call. Frank had recently received his master's degree from Columbia University and was working as a researcher in the American History Room of the New York Public Library when he began having trouble with his vision. Unable to find the cause of his sudden problem and fearful of losing his sight permanently, Frank decided to go to Minnesota to be treated by the only doctor he truly trusted. And Archie gave him good news: With an extended period of rest, the blurriness would eventually disappear. So for the next few months, Alecia helped Frank take some of the strain off his eyes by reading the newspaper aloud to him while Doc was at work.

She also helped nurse Frank back to health after a freak midwinter incident in which he nearly died from falling through the ice while walking across a lake he thought was completely frozen. Alecia and her brother-in-law grew close during the time Frank stayed in Chisholm. He remained there even after his eyesight returned to normal, leaving in April 1917 only after being accepted into the United States Marines. Later, after he became president of the University of North Carolina, Frank often traveled to Minnesota to visit and vacation.

Sadly, Archie never got the chance to spend more time with David, a member of the first Marine Corps detachment to go across the Atlantic with General Black Jack Pershing to

Doc and Alecia, along with three of their tenants, lived in this house on Second Avenue in Chisholm. The Grahams' apartment was downstairs on the right. The foundation of the A-frame house was purportedly made from smooth, round stones from Lake Superior.

PHOTO BY BRETT FRIEDLANDER

fight the Germans in World War I. As his brother's designated next of kin, he was the first family member to learn of David's death on June 6, 1918, during the Battle of Belleau Wood in the Château-Thierry region of France. The loss of his older brother and kindred spirit affected Archie deeply. Shortly after David was killed, Doc attempted to enlist for military service, too, only to be turned down because of his age and a variety of health issues.

Heartbroken that he was unable to help finish the job his brother had started, Archie did whatever he could back home to honor David and aid the war effort. Years later when World War II broke out, he made it a point to be at the local Greyhound station anytime Chisholm boys went away to serve their country. He would shake their hands, thank them for their dedication, and wish them luck. When World War II was over and Chisholm held a celebration for its returning heroes, Graham shed tears—both of joy and of sorrow for those like his brother who never made it home—as he rode on one of the floats.

Because David's death affected Doc so profoundly, younger brother Frank hoped that the traumatic event would convince the family's resident doctor to leave frozen Minnesota and return home to the Carolinas. But Archie had become too woven into the fabric of Chisholm by that time to consider such a move. Later in life, after Frank retired from public service and moved in with his sister Kate—who became something of a caretaker for him—the two would take walks through their neighborhood and talk about their baseball-playing brother who had somehow drifted so far away from their once close-knit family. Since Archie had recently retired, too, they dreamed he would surprise them by showing up at their door and saying, "I'm here," the way he had done at the Rood Hospital in 1909. It never happened.

While Doc remained distant from his own family, he interacted much more closely with the Maddens. He was particularly fond of a nephew, Bob, who spent several summers with the Grahams in Chisholm. At least twice a year, Doc and Alecia would get in their old LaSalle and drive south to Rochester. While he attended medical conferences or met with colleagues at the Mayo Clinic, she stayed with her sister Jen and spent all day shopping for antiques and jewelry. "That's where she was in her element," Bob Madden's wife, Nan, later recalled. "I met her a couple of times by chance in antique stores and she was like, 'Oh, did you see this?' and 'Oh, did you see that?' and I don't know how much she bought. Lots. Lots. Lots. I remember one time she bought so much stuff that they had to have it shipped up to Chisholm."

It didn't matter that they usually lacked a place to put all the things Alecia bought. Or that most of the time she barely had enough money to pay for it all. She got it anyway. As a result, the Graham home ended up looking like a warehouse full of items waiting to be displayed at a museum.

Doc and Alecia lived in a large, comfortable house they had built for them a few years after they married. The foundation was made of smooth, round stones from Lake Superior. Or at least that's what Graham believed. According to local legend, the group of high-school students Doc paid to fetch the stones didn't feel like going all the way to Duluth to get them, so they picked them out of a nearby mine quarry, and no one ever knew the difference. Instead of building up on Windy Hill "with the high-and-mighty"—as longtime friend and Chisholm High basketball coach Bob McDonald described some of the local citizens—the Grahams decided to live among the common folk down in Pig Town. Located at the corner of Second Avenue and Sixth Street, two blocks from the new Washington School, their house was divided into four apartments separated by a central foyer and a distinctive A-frame entry. The Grahams lived in the largest unit, downstairs on the right. It had three bedrooms, a living room, a dining room with a stone fireplace, one bathroom, a small kitchen, and a pantry.

In one of the bedrooms, used primarily for storage, five Oriental rugs were piled one on top of the other on the floor. Standing on a crowded tabletop like tin soldiers guarding the crown jewels were rows of silver candlesticks, which Alecia bought by the dozen. Against one of the walls, boxes of china that had never been opened were piled almost to the ceiling. Other sets of dishes were displayed in hutches and breakfronts strategically located throughout the house. Amid all the clutter was a baby grand piano Alecia played for her Docky in the evenings when he got home from work.

As different as they were in temperament and upbringing, the two were in many ways the perfect couple. They had their individual quirks but accepted each other without hesitation. Like his father, Doc was fidgety and impatient and had a tendency to say whatever was on his mind, no matter what the consequences. Alecia was a quiet, nurturing woman who usually ended up being her husband's social conscience.

An example of this came during the Great Depression when the Grahams decided to spend a warm Sunday afternoon together outdoors. Alecia packed a picnic lunch, and Doc, as he often did, employed a local teenager to drive them out of town to one of the many small lakes that dotted the landscape around Chisholm. Bob "Bogey" Dicklich eagerly accepted the job. But as he stood by the car while the Grahams enjoyed their luxurious spread of fried chicken and other delicacies, his stomach began to rumble. "I'm sitting there hungrier than a son-of-a-gun," he recalled.

Finally, Alecia began to feel guilty. "Docky, why don't you give the kid a little something?" she said.

"[Working class] people aren't used to this kind of food," he replied, chewing on a drumstick. "Give him an apple."

Alecia did. Then, with a disapproving look, she made her husband give Dicklich a piece of chicken, too.

As the years went on, the Grahams began to live separate lives. By day, the two rarely saw one another after Doc put on his trademark black coat and hat and stepped out the door before the crack of dawn for his daily walk. His usual routine was to stop at Pappas Bakery & Candy Kitchen for his morning coffee and donut. Then he'd often meet up with Gertrude Haller, the German teacher at Chisholm High School, and walk across the Bridge of Peace—the long man-made causeway that dissected Longyear Lake—and back before heading off to work. Once school was over, Doc made house calls, checked on children absent from school, hung out at his friend Andrew Niemalla's garage, or even snuck over to the park to watch and sometimes help the boys play baseball. He returned home around dinnertime, usually after dark.

Alecia, on the other hand, usually spent her days at home. When she did venture out of the house, she dressed as though she were going to church on Sunday. She favored blue, lavender, and other pastel colors and always wore a hat and plenty of jewelry. And she was elegant enough to pull it off without looking pretentious. In the afternoons, a group of her friends, mostly the wives of teachers and coaches, came over to socialize and play bridge. Alecia was particularly close to her cousin J. P.'s wife, Leathe. The two did virtually everything together, especially when it came to helping the children in the Chisholm school system. At the end of every school year, the two women put on a lavish dinner for all the members of Chisholm's faculty and their families.

Though Doc and Alecia were not often seen together in public, they were rarely apart in the evenings after he got home. "They were kind of cloistered in a way," Bob McDonald said. "Alecia never needed much. She was content with the way Doc was, because he'd always come home. He was never a philanderer or anything of that nature. He was just a good fellow. Their whole existence was each other, really."

It was a codependence that became a necessity when Alecia found out she couldn't bear children. The bad news hit her hard. Having come from a large family, Alecia dreamed of someday having a houseful of her own offspring to love and raise. But it just wasn't to be. Initially, she turned to her husband for comfort. What he couldn't give her, she found in Leathe Vaughan, a natural confidant who shared her inability to conceive. Eventually, the reality of her infertility set in, and Alecia and Doc began sharing their love and affection with all the children of Chisholm. In effect, they made the next four decades of youngsters their unofficially adopted sons and daughters, providing them with guidance, generosity, jobs, and healthcare. In some cases, they even financed students' college educations.

Doc always tried to keep coins and candy such as lemon drops in his pocket so he could give them to children he met along the street during his frequent walks through town. Knowing this, the youngsters followed him around like the Pied Piper. Doc made them work for their reward by tossing the candy or money into the grass, taking great pleasure in watching them scramble to pick it all up.

To help fill the void in her life, Alecia sought direction and strength from the young priest at Chisholm's Catholic church, St. Joseph's. Monsignor John Schifferer came to town in 1911. Like many others, including the Grahams, he formed a bond with the community, staying for 60 years. He didn't just serve as a dedicated spiritual adviser to Alecia. He also helped provide her the creative outlet she had been missing by putting

Downtown Chisholm as seen from across the Bridge of Freedom. One of Doc's routines was to walk across the bridge and up Lake Street to have coffee and a donut at Pappas Bakery & Candy Kitchen on his way to school each morning.
COURTESY OF THE CITY OF CHISHOLM, MINNESOTA

her in charge of the church's annual St. Patrick's Day show. The plays were always spectacular productions, ranging from Rudyard Kipling's epic *The Gypsy Trail* to the farcical comedy *The Patsy*. Despite their affiliation with the church, the shows were held at the public high school, where they played to appreciative standing-room-only crowds in the 1,445-seat auditorium. And sitting by himself on the aisle in the back row of the main floor was her proud husband. Although Monsignor Schifferer always presented Alecia with an engraved silver tray as a token of his appreciation for her hard work, her favorite reward was the dozen red roses Docky lovingly gave her at the end of each show.

Graham took great pleasure in lavishing his wife with gifts. He made it a point to buy her something new every chance he could, whether a gift as simple as another blue hat he saw in a Lake Street storefront or her two most prized possessions, the pair of diamond rings that would become known as "the family jewels." One was an engagement ring set with a .87-carat white, clear diamond. The other was a 1.54-carat dinner ring Doc bought for Alecia after they had been married for several years. She never left the house without wearing them. "Alecia loved jewelry, and she had a presence to carry it," her great-niece Lynn Didier recalled.

Doc wasn't interested in such frivolities as jewelry, fashion, and furnishings. He never even bothered to wear a wedding band. Alecia's most frequent gifts to him were her love, trust, and understanding. Of the three, the last was by far the most important because of her husband's long hours and sometimes absent-minded behavior. It wasn't unusual for Alecia's afternoon bridge game to be interrupted by a phone call from a tenant at one of the Grahams' many rental properties. Knowing that Docky probably wouldn't get around to fixing the leaky toilet or broken door for several weeks, if at all,

Alecia would take it upon herself to do the job for him. First, she would politely serve her guests coffee or tea. Then she'd excuse herself to take care of the pressing business. What a sight the gentle little woman with the blue dress, hat, and jewelry must have been as she hurried down the sidewalk on her thick legs and high heels, waving a 15-inch pipe wrench in her hand as she went to fix a toilet!

Or at least to try to fix it.

As educated as Alecia was, her technical knowledge was severely limited. Once, on one of their many trips to Rochester, the Grahams' old Cadillac began smoking like an incinerator before rolling to a stop with transmission problems somewhere on Center Street. While Doc looked under the hood to determine what was wrong, he told his wife to find a pay phone and call her sisters. "Tell them we're going to be late because the car is dead on Center," he said.

Being the good wife she was, Alecia did just that. But somehow she misunderstood the message. Instead of a street, she thought that "Center" was part of the car. So from that day on, anytime something went wrong with the vehicle, her diagnosis was always the same. "It's probably the Center again," she'd say. Doc would usually just smile and tell her she was probably right.

Alecia was just as tolerant of him—to a point, at least. On those rare occasions when they fought, it was usually about money—specifically, Doc's handling of it. Nothing irritated her more than finding an uncashed rent check lying around the house or learning after the fact that her husband had bankrolled a group of local boys who wanted to drive down to Minneapolis to see the Chisholm High basketball or baseball team play in the state tournament. That's why Doc often waited until Alecia was out of town before making a major expenditure, such as funding a postseason banquet for all the school's coaches. Eventually, she'd find out about it and wouldn't be happy. But she rarely, if ever, let Doc know that she knew.

That was just the way they were. Right or wrong, good or bad, Doc and Alecia always backed each other up, right to the very end. In 1963, after his retirement from medicine, Graham ran a successful campaign and was elected to the Chisholm School Board. When he died three years later, Alecia stepped in to serve out the remainder of his four-year term. Because of her educational background and the inner beauty she retained long after her distinctive dark-chocolate hair turned white, she seemed a natural fit for the position. "She really wasn't a public personality," said Jim Vitali, a fellow member of the board. "She played the part of the doctor's wife, but she was a proud lady, and everyone in town admired her." Even after all that time away from the classroom, the dainty Miss Flower was still as beloved as ever.

CHAPTER 8

Chisholm's Guardian
Caring and Compassion for All

"His kindness is one of his most outstanding qualities and during his past years in Chisholm, he has surely shown much of it."

DEDICATION TO DR. GRAHAM,
1951 CHISHOLM HIGH YEARBOOK

ALTHOUGH HE WAS HIRED to care for what one authority called "the sick and weary bodies of the miners" of the Iron Range, Doc Graham grew increasingly immersed in and fascinated by the ills of their children. The typhoid epidemic of 1910, coming within months of his arrival, was the first catastrophe to advance him toward that preference. Four years later, tragedy again left its mark on Graham's adopted city. A polio epidemic struck Chisholm. In the words of one local resident, "Many babies died that year." Why the adolescent and adult populations weren't hit as hard by the crippling and often fatal affliction remains a mystery. Graham once again used his skills to ease suffering and to help rid the city of a dreaded ailment.

The doctor who never missed a day of work in 44 years hardly had time to complete his treatment of polio cases when a third plague reared its ugly head. In 1916, a diphtheria epidemic that rose to 200 cases swept through Chisholm. Dr. Graham again worked tirelessly, particularly among the young, trying to contain a devastating disease.

The expertise he gained during the crisis and those that preceded it served him well when he was hired in the summer of 1917 to become the Chisholm school system's first full-time physician. With his beloved bride of two years providing support, he not only accepted his routine duties but also created and welcomed previously unheard-of assignments. In addition to his school assignments, Doc continued to see patients on the side. He stopped by their homes to examine children and adults alike in the afternoons following school. When his phone rang at night with someone on the other end complaining of a stomachache, a high fever, or a baby with croup, he grabbed his little black bag and headed out the door, no questions asked. And usually he did it without asking for anything in return.

Graham was energized by a newfound confidence in his own health. In 1915, on the eve of his wedding, Graham had traveled to Rochester for a thorough physical examination. He had especially sought assurance that the respiratory ailment that had taken him to the Iron Range six years earlier was no longer a threat to either his life or the professional challenges for which he yearned. The results of his extended stay at the Mayo Clinic were pleasing. "The doctors here have examined me and are unable to find any ailment," he reported in an affectionate letter to Alecia.

To ensure that the news would remain good, Doc became

as conscious of his personal health as he was of the well-being of his young patients. At times, he took things to the point of obsession, like when he would walk around town making a purring noise by blowing air through his mouth, believing that the ritual helped keep his lungs clear. Maybe there was a method to his madness. He remained athletic and physically fit, often amazing the teenage boys at the high school with his feats of throwing and hitting long after his official playing days were over.

He needed to stay sharp, too, because despite all his good works, the boys were constantly trying to put one over on their kindhearted doctor. One of their favorite tricks was the fake pinkeye epidemic. It usually began in the spring when the weather finally started to improve and every young man's fancy turned to, among other things, baseball. In order to get out of the classroom and onto the field early, junior class president Jim Vitali and a group of his friends would bring an onion to school. At the appropriate time, they would rub the juice from the onion into their eyes and ask their teachers if they could go see Doc Graham.

It was a good plan, except that Graham prided himself in being Chisholm's unofficial truant officer. Every evening on his way home from school, he would parade around the neighborhood checking up on those children who had been absent that day. Some parents who couldn't afford medical care actually kept their children out of school in order to elicit free house calls. But not Vitali and his friends. The last thing they wanted was an after-hours visit from the school doctor. Still, they took the gamble, hoping that Graham's love for the sport outweighed his devotion to public service. "He knew we were going down to the field to play," Vitali said. "But he'd sign us out and let us go anyway." A few hours later, when school was over, Graham would often show up to watch the games or even play a little if one of the sides needed an extra man. He never forgot the lure and joy of the national pastime.

Graham's love for sports went far beyond baseball. As a former major leaguer and big-time college football player, he was equally enamored with those who played football, basketball, and just about everything else for the Blue Streaks of Chisholm High. He often amazed the young players with feats of his own athleticism, including throwing a baseball some 335 feet on the fly from home plate over the left-field fence at the school field. "He could throw it a mile," former Chisholm High athlete and basketball coach Bob McDonald remembered. That accomplishment was included by W. P. Kinsella in *Shoeless Joe*. Doc was equally adept at throwing a football, though according to those who knew him, he had an unconventional way of doing it. "He would put the ball with one point in his palm and the other in the bend of his elbow, and he'd throw that thing," former student Fred Lautizi said. "It would come out spinning [vertically] instead of a spiral. He would say, 'This is the way we did it in the good old days.'"

Not only did Graham become the town's biggest athletic booster, he also served as the high school's unofficial team doctor. He made sure to bring oranges and apples, which he bought by the crate, to every game. He accompanied the boys on the bus for as many road games as he could. When the Blue Streaks won or gave a heroic effort, Doc would reach into his pocket and give each player a 50-cent piece. "That meant an awful lot to those boys, because 50 cents was a lot more then than it is now," newspaper publisher Veda Ponikvar said.

During the games, Doc would stalk the sidelines wearing his trademark hat and long black coat, cheering the boys on. He elicited shrugs from confused onlookers when he began using unfamiliar terms such as "proper hydration" while handing out orange slices to the boys playing ball for the Blue

Doc Graham in the late 1920s or early 1930s
COURTESY OF THE LYNN WILLIAMSON DIDIER COLLECTION

Streaks. When somebody went down with an injury, he'd grab his medical bag, jog onto the field or court, and administer first aid. In essence, he was among the first doctors in the country to practice what is now known as sports medicine. "Kids today are healthier in every respect," he told the *Duluth News-Tribune* in July 1952. "They're taller and weigh more and [have] got more brains in their heads than we ever had. I wouldn't worry about them so long as they live right."

For his part, Doc did everything in his power to make sure they did. His treatment methods, however, were anything but revolutionary. With the exception of sprained ankles and knees that needed wrapping, Graham's first response to most maladies was to pull out a cotton swab, dip it into a bottle of Mercurochrome, and brush it on the affected area. "What it was, really, was a placebo," Bob McDonald said. "Young kids responded to that. I don't care what [the injury] was. If you turned an ankle or got a cramp on the football field, he'd pull out that Mercurochrome and swab you up. I'm sure he knew [that it didn't do anything medically], but as a kid, he'd put it on you and you always thought you were better."

The remedy worked just as well in Graham's everyday practice. He used it whenever a student came to his office complaining of a sore throat, a stomachache, or anything else. The routine was always the same. He'd listen to the children's hearts and lungs, take a look down their throats, swab them, and send them on their way. The treatment didn't always make the patient feel better. It did, however, prove an effective deterrent to unnecessary trips to the doctor and missed class time. No student, unless truly sick, ever wanted to have their tonsils painted with Mercurochrome.

Not all of the good doctor's diagnoses were so simplistic or easily dismissed. When he was less than a year into his tenure with the school system, yet another epidemic swept into

Chisholm. This one was by far the most frightening to date—a virus that killed 50 million people worldwide, among them thousands of American youngsters. The city and its school system were ready, however. Thanks in large measure to the transplanted Tar Heel who introduced an inoculation program for his students, few youngsters became victims. That doesn't mean his efforts were accepted without a measure of skepticism and scorn. "Parents were suspicious at first," Graham told a reporter from the *Duluth News-Tribune* in 1952. "[They were] afraid we'd poison their kids."

Sensing the virulence of the 1918 flu, Graham prevailed upon Dr. Vaughan to convert the local schools into temporary hospitals. Mary Norsberg, delivered by Graham in 1912, was only six at the time. But 85 years later, in 1997, she still remembered how Graham moved from bed to bed and patient to patient, easing pain, uttering calm words of confidence, and using unusual flu-fighting strategies. Among them: wearing braids of garlic, whose foul smell provided pungent, potent opposition to the contagion.

Despite the early objections, Graham convinced a majority of residents to go along with the injections. His efforts were rewarded with the respect of an entire community once it realized the benefits of his preventive treatment. The great flu epidemic of 1918 that proved so devastating elsewhere took few young lives in Chisholm. Because of Graham's efforts, the city escaped the quarantines that were commonplace in dozens of urban areas from Connecticut to California. In fact, not once during Graham's 44 years of service with the school system was Chisholm ever quarantined because of communicable diseases.

Once the flu epidemic subsided, Graham turned his attention to less dramatic ways of showing his commitment to Chisholm's little ones. When he sensed an unaddressed medical need, he aggressively confronted it without worrying about the consequences. For instance, he was quick to observe that tooth care was virtually nonexistent on the Iron Range and that, as a result, rotting teeth led quickly and commonly to full dentures. Such a sequence would prove unnecessary, he concluded, if youth were introduced to brushing their teeth immediately upon entering school. With Superintendent Vaughan's unqualified support, Graham not only outfitted each student with his or her own toothbrush but also required that it be put to daily use. "Brushing became part of the regular school day," reported one observer years later.

Doc's office was in the Washington School only about two blocks from his home on Second Avenue. It had two desks—a roll top for Doc and a more conventional one for his nurse. Each morning, Graham would lean over the old roll top and share a "thought of the day" with one of the many nurses who assisted him throughout his career. Occasionally, a secretary would join the two to transcribe notes and file paperwork. Virtually everything in the room, including the chairs, was painted the same government-issue olive green, giving the place an antiseptically impersonal look and feel. Though he was always quick with a smile, a quip, or one of his customary queries—"How's your mudda?" or "Is your fadda working?"—Graham didn't care much about improving the atmosphere. Other than his trusty eye chart, the only thing that resembled a decoration on the walls was a poster promoting good posture. One side showed a man hunched over just like the animals he trailed; the caption read, "If man walked like animals . . ." The other side showed the man walking upright behind an elephant and a giraffe; the words said, "If animals walked like man . . ."

Graham was just as attuned to his students' social welfare as he was to their physical development. He recognized that certain aspects of their lives required more than a swab of his trusty Mercurochrome. Among his favorite times was Halloween. Every year, he got one of the boys from the high school to drive him to the nearby town of Balkin to pick up a black cat, which he would put into the pocket of his cape-like overcoat. Then he would go from classroom to classroom in the elementary school to show the children. "Some of the youngsters really enjoyed the cat, while others shied away," recalled nurse Frances Russ. "Either way, Dr. Graham would enjoy their response."

He got an even bigger kick out of attending to the needs of the older kids, especially when they included such important life moments as the junior prom. Jim Vitali learned that firsthand in the spring of 1950. As the junior-class president, he had the responsibility of presiding over the festivities in the gymnasium. But because he didn't have enough money to rent a tuxedo and buy a corsage, dinner, and other necessities for the evening, he decided that it would probably be best to spend a quiet evening at home with his parents. Besides, he didn't have a girlfriend to invite, and with the hour of the dance rapidly approaching, his prospects for a last-minute date were slim at best.

That is, until Graham learned his plight. Recognizing that the junior-class president should not be a no-show at his own prom, Doc sent word to Vitali on the afternoon of the affair that he needed to see him in his school office. Upon reporting, Vitali was surprised to learn that Doc had been at work on his behalf. Graham had procured a corsage, arranged for dinner—the whole works! He even found a girl. "If you want to go," he told Vitali, "I will take care of everything." The befuddled youngster sputtered and stuttered, so surprised was he that no detail had gone unattended. Finally, he composed himself enough to accept the offer.

It turned out to be a memorable evening for Vitali. In the company of Lois Nessola, the attractive daughter of the school janitor, and with $25 in his pocket "to cover my expenses," he rode to and from the prom in a "nice, big car" driven by Daniel Klein, a doctor's son, whose date was as stunning as his own. "A magnificent experience," was how Vitali later described the event, made possible by a man he later proclaimed to be "a wonderful person and a fine gentleman."

Doc played no favorites, befriending females as readily and as often as he did boys. Mary Vecchi Russo's dramatic recovery from rickets, the bone-deforming ailment so tragically prevalent in the first decade of the 20th century, illustrated how Graham acknowledged no obstacles to returning "his" youngsters to health.

Born in Luxembourg, Mary contracted rickets just prior to her family's arrival on the Iron Range shortly after the end of World War I. It worsened as the result of the poverty that kept her and her two siblings from what she called "the right food." An older sister had also contracted the disease but had been lucky enough to have it corrected by surgery when she was three, before the Vecchis immigrated to the United States. The move used up most of the family's savings, though, so they were unable to afford the expensive operations needed to straighten Mary's crooked legs. As she grew into adolescence, she became convinced that only the grave would cure her of the embarrassing, debilitating effects of her rickets. She wore pants to school—unheard of at the time for girls—in an attempt to hide her abnormality.

Graham envisioned a different, normal future for the otherwise attractive miner's daughter. He was moved to action in 1931 after learning that the high-school sophomore had failed to gain a role in the school play because, after tryouts, the drama teacher spied her deformed legs for the first time. The

"Doc"

With a wee bit of effort, I think I can,
Compose a little verse about a wonderful man.
We all know him as dear "Doc" Graham.
He knows any child, and he knows the name.
His coat pockets bulge from candy and gum.
For some little child he calls his chum.
The children love him and so do we all.
Always so gentle when out on sick call.
Comes Halloween he's a clown or maybe a witch,
Whatever has to be done, he's there to pitch.
Years ago it was a baseball for the Miami's he threw.
And he didn't continue, for what would we do,
Without Dr. Graham, who we love and respect.
As Chisholm's favorite Doctor, you we select.
You are as gentle as a kitten, and cherished like a rose.
The man with many friends, I'm sure you have no foes.
If I could make a wish, I know what I would say.
Please, dear Doctor Graham, don't ever go away.

Marge Podlogar

Poem written by Chisholm High student Marge Podlogar in honor of Doc Graham during the late 1950s
COURTESY OF THE LYNN WILLIAMSON DIDIER COLLECTION

aspiring young actress knew she had lost the part by the tone of her teacher's voice the moment she said, "Mary, I've got to talk to you." Devastated, Mary began crying before she was even given the bad news. Thankfully, the teacher was sensitive to Mary's hurt feelings. But that didn't change anything. She reluctantly explained that parading rickets-bent legs on stage would prove distracting to audiences. Another girl replaced Mary in the cast.

When word of what happened reached Dr. Graham, he vowed to provide Mary the medical attention she needed. With a few phone calls to the Gillette State Children's Hospital in Minneapolis, he arranged for one of his colleagues to perform the surgeries. Convincing Mary's proud father to accept the help wasn't as easy. Struggling financially during the depths of the Great Depression, Mr. Vecchi was having a hard enough time supporting his family without taking on the burden of costly operations. Many times, the only food the Vecchis had to eat was the blueberries they picked off the bushes surrounding their home in the mining camp of Dunwoody, just outside the city limits.

Doc approached Mary's father repeatedly over the course of a month but was rebuffed each time. The family just didn't have enough money, Mr. Vecchi would tell him. Graham's persistence finally paid off when he convinced the stubborn miner that he would need to provide nothing more than permission for his daughter's treatment. The doctor himself would take care of transporting Mary to "the Cities" by allowing her to ride along when he accompanied the Chisholm High basketball squad to the state tournament. Financing, he fibbed, was unnecessary because Gillette was a state hospital where "everything was paid for."

One of the demands of the lengthy, painful surgeries was that Mary's legs be placed in vices, broken, and reset. She spent nearly five months in the hospital. Decades later, she recalled that Doc was nearly as excited about her new look as she was upon her return home. "He wanted to see my legs," she explained. "He'd shout out, 'Aren't they so lovely? They're so beautiful!' "

The expenses for the medical procedures and ensuing hospitalization remained forever hidden. The school physician quietly provided for them from his own earnings. Small wonder, then, that for the rest of her long and happy life, Mary considered the North Carolina native "the kindest, sweetest person I've ever met." Small wonder, too, that throughout her adulthood, she sent $25 each month to help reimburse the Gillette State Children's Hospital "for what Doc Graham did for me. That's the only way I could really think to repay him," she said.

Doc's generosity and caring made him beloved to nearly everybody in the community. One such example was related by barber Frank Tancabel, who remembered driving to the Twin Cities with some friends to watch Chisholm High's basketball team play in the state tournament. After their expenses for gas and motel rooms, the boys were left without any money. Doc ran into them the morning of the game and asked if they had eaten. The looks on their faces told him all he needed to know. "Here's money for you," Tancabel recalled Graham saying as he handed over whatever he had in his pocket. "Now, you can have breakfast."

"Doc Graham was a father figure to every kid that came through this school for a long, long time," said Rita Costanzi-Charter, the librarian at Chisholm High. "He was the kind of person you wish we still had more of here. To have someone like that to learn from is a benefit you can't put a value on."

One of Doc's greatest rewards came when he heard of youngsters from Chisholm who went on to become successful in their chosen fields. He remembered all of them by name and often bragged about them to others whenever he traveled back east or to medical conferences outside the Iron Range. And he had plenty to brag about. According to Veda Ponikvar, Chisholm produced an average of one medical doctor a year between 1912 and the mid-1990s, many, if not most, of them influenced by their now-famous role model.

Among the most successful was Dr. Walter Bowe, who spent 46 years as a surgeon and professor of anatomy at Notre Dame and the Wake Forest University Medical Center in Winston-Salem, North Carolina. When Bowe was a fourth-grader, Graham may have saved his life when he discovered a heart murmur during a routine school physical. He immediately told Bowe's parents to take him to see a specialist at the hospital in Duluth. "As it turned out, the valves in my heart weren't closing right," Bowe recalled. "They told me not to exercise at all for a year, and everything turned out all right." During that period, Bowe realized what he wanted to do when he grew up. "I adored Dr. Graham," he said. "Even now, I tell my students that they should be caring people, just like him."

CHAPTER 9

Uncuffed
The Big Leagues of Medical Research

———

*"His masterpiece was the blood pressure data,
compiled over a 30-year span and involving
50,000 children."*

IHMBRA MASONIC MAGAZINE,
APRIL 1993

BY TODAY'S MEDICAL STANDARDS, it would be a benign request.

"Would it be possible and would permission be granted," Doc Graham asked his best friend and boss, J. P. Vaughan, shortly before school started in the fall of 1926, "for me to take the blood pressures of children from K to 12 in the Chisholm schools?"

It was a question that could easily have been answered by another question: Why?

At that time, no one had ever seen the need to monitor the blood pressures of minors. A few doctors had tried, but the studies were inconclusive because their techniques weren't uniform and the students they used were too few in number for comprehensive statistical conclusions. Not that it really mattered. Anyone who was anyone in the medical field believed that hypertension and its related complications were afflictions confined to adults. Those who disagreed were dismissed as quacks.

Why Graham risked public ridicule and professional disdain isn't quite certain. Maybe he was just curious, as had been the case a few years earlier when he researched and experimented in an unsuccessful attempt to determine how aspirin worked. Or perhaps he simply needed something to keep him busy during those long idle hours between hearing tests and Mercurochrome swabbings. More likely, he'd noticed something in one of his young patients that piqued his curiosity or stimulated his deep-seated interest in research. Whatever the case, he held his breath as he walked into the superintendent's office that August morning to make his unorthodox request.

His fears, however, were quickly eased by the smile on Dr. Vaughan's face as he pondered the question. "Doc," Vaughan replied, "this is your program. You are the doctor. You do what you need to make the program a success."

It was exactly what Graham wanted to hear. Accompanying the positive words was an offer to assist the physician in gaining approval from the school board. Thus, within days, Doc won formal permission from the group legally charged with overseeing Chisholm's schools. Soon thereafter, he began the 15-year study that eventually involved 3,580 children, followed year by year from the age of five to 16. A later medical journal noted that "25,000 [children's blood pressure] determinations made by one physician with a constant technique and under identical circumstance" had never before been attempted.

This would become the lasting legacy of Graham's lifetime dedication to medicine and the children he served. The results of his study became so well known and respected that they were cited in medical textbooks for decades to come. To this day, the study remains on file for researchers to use at the Mayo Clinic.

To the children of Chisholm, it was just another reason to get out of class. "We always used to look forward to it," said Angelo Vittori, a former student to whom Graham took a particular liking. "He would line the kids up outside his office, and we'd all have a good time while we waited for it to be our turn. I don't think we really understood what we were doing, but we didn't care."

Blood pressure is the force blood exerts against its vessel walls as the heart pumps. It increases when the heart contracts, pushing blood through the circulatory system, and lowers when the heart relaxes. It is affected by activity, rest, body temperature, emotional state, and other factors. When a child has high blood pressure, the heart must pump harder, and the arteries have a much heavier work load. Such a condition, if left untreated, can have an adverse effect on organs including the brain and kidneys.

Once a month, Graham would summon the children by class. One at a time, he'd sit them down, fit a cuff around their arm, and pump it up. Then, as he slowly let the air escape, he'd listen with a stethoscope and call out numbers for his nurse to write down. The first persistent sound that he heard was the systolic blood pressure. The second indicated the diastolic pressure. If a child seemed nervous or excited at the time of the test, Graham didn't take a reading until he or she could be calmed down, in order to protect the consistency of the results. After every child in the school was tested, Doc gave the raw data to his part-time assistant, Mary Giannini, who transcribed and cataloged it all. This continued for years. As

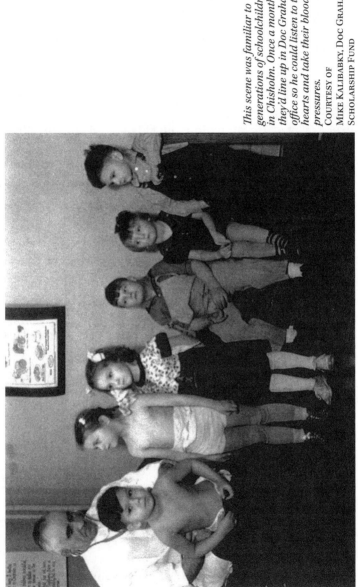

This scene was familiar to generations of schoolchildren in Chisholm. Once a month, they'd line up in Doc Graham's office so he could listen to their hearts and take their blood pressures.

the first group of children grew up and graduated, they were replaced by new subjects just beginning their school experience.

But what did all those numbers mean? More importantly, what should he do with them?

Those were questions Doc asked frequently during his regular trips to the Mayo Clinic in Rochester. At a conference in 1941, he was introduced to Robert P. Gage and Dr. Edgar A. Hines, Jr., who finally helped him find the answers he sought.

Gage was a brilliant man. The 20th century produced few medical statisticians more competent and better respected. The Mayo Clinic was fortunate to have his services for 27 years—from 1937, when he left a lucrative post with an Indiana investment company, until his premature death at age 50 in 1964. He was so respected that an elementary school was named in his honor in Rochester. Even more accomplished and better known was Hines, who earned his M.D. in 1928 from the Medical College of South Carolina in Charleston and joined the Mayo Clinic as an instructor in 1935. By the start of World War II, Dr. Hines was acknowledged as one of the world's foremost authorities on blood pressure ailments.

Neither he nor Gage, though, had ever seen data like Graham brought to their attention. It startled and impressed them both. It had originally been dismissed as a waste of time by many, including the citizens of Chisholm, who predicted that Doc was destined for disappointment. But Gage and Hines believed otherwise. So did the Josiah Macy, Jr., Foundation of New York, which provided a grant of over $5,000 to assist with the expenses the trio was certain to incur while assessing Graham's data.

Their findings weren't as earth-shattering as they were informative. For one thing, the revelation that "much hypertension was found" among Doc's students ran contrary to commonly held notions about high blood pressure in children. More importantly, for the first time anywhere, the study identified and set normal standards for youngsters ages five through 16. In Graham's words, the results showed "an apparent increase in the variability of blood pressure for the entire group with increasing age. The changes became especially evident at about puberty and continued during adolescence. The variation of blood pressure was greater for girls at the ages of 10, 11, 12 and 13 years than for boys at these ages. The mean systolic blood pressure ranged from 92 at age 5 to 122 at the age of 16."

Doc's undertaking caught the attention of the entire medical profession. Appearing in the April 1945 *American Journal of Diseases of Children,* the findings of the doctor from the "small city" of Chisholm proved so valuable that the five-page article quickly became required reading for every prospective M.D. in every medical school across the globe. Graham's alliance with the Mayo Clinic undoubtedly aided in earning the article international attention. Mayo, Gage, and Hines were names over which no medical practitioner could fail to pause. Yet listed first, immediately below the title of the essay, was Archibald W. Graham, M.D., the man who had put forward the proof that children—even the very young—could and did suffer from high blood pressure.

Ironically, Graham had no idea his work was so universally respected. It wasn't until his brother Frank, a United States senator living in Washington at the time, happened upon the study in a textbook in 1950 that Doc finally became fully aware of its impact.

The awards and recognition rolled in. First, he was invited to present his findings to the members of the Minnesota Medical Association in 1957. The following summer, he received an even greater honor when he was selected to lecture his fellow doctors about children's blood pressures at the national convention of the American Medical Association. On June 11, 1958, at Northwestern University in Chicago, Chisholm's Doc Graham told the more than 14,000 physicians in attendance that "the prevailing notion that children don't get high blood pressure is erroneous." That conclusion was met with an ovation. On his way home, Graham was given the opportunity to stop at the Mayo Clinic and witness what the *Chisholm Tribune-Herald* referred to as "a modern operation" on a child's heart. "The surgeon made it look like an ordinary operation," an amazed Graham told the newspaper.

Although he continued to take blood pressure readings for the rest of his career with the school system, Graham never published again. It's not that he didn't want to. In his famous article, he promised to take up other blood-pressure-related subjects "in a subsequent paper." But because he used all the money he had received from the Macy Foundation, and because others, including researchers at the Mayo Clinic, began undertaking their own studies, further publication was not necessary. Nonetheless, his lone public paper catapulted the North Carolina native to the kind of notoriety in the medical field he never achieved on the baseball diamond. It also proved what the citizens of Chisholm already knew—that he loved children.

Children on every continent and in every nation were the beneficiaries of Graham's 1945 study. It was so accurate and so thorough that almost a half-century later, Dr. Sol Londe of the Washington University School of Medicine in St. Louis referred to it in his article "Blood Pressure in Children As Determined Under Office Conditions," published in the September 1990 issue of *Clinical Pediatrics* magazine.

Gage provided the correlations and analyses of variance and Hines the interpretations related to systolic and diastolic blood pressures. The foundation on which their work rested was the data and hypothesis of Archibald W. Graham, M.D. It was a contribution of love.

CHAPTER 10

Weird Science
Chewed Paper, Uncashed Checks,
and the Search for Perpetual Motion

⌒

"He was part philanthropist, part mad scientist."
Friend and colleague
Dr. Woodrow "Woody"
Anderson

His was a mind that, like poet Walt Whitman's, contained "multitudes." And if like Whitman he contradicted himself or common sense, he neither sulked nor wavered. Doc Graham envisioned possibilities that escaped conventional thinkers and devoted countless hours attempting to bring them to reality.

Such was the case with his study that changed the thinking about children's blood pressures. But Chisholm's unconventional school doctor was inspired by more than just medical science. In his heart, Graham saw himself not merely as a healer and serious researcher but also as an inventor *extraordinaire*. He was no less inclined to consider the scientifically bizarre than he was to put a cuff around a youngster's arm and listen for a reading.

From his earliest days, he yearned to do something profound with his life and, like his well-known father, earn the respect and adulation of those around him. The only question was how he would do it. Baseball once held that possibility. Medicine, too, had been no less promising. But neither, nor both together, had led him anywhere but the proverbial middle of nowhere.

To say Doc Graham was quirky is like saying it gets cold in the winter in northern Minnesota. "He was something different," Angelo Vittori said. The people of Chisholm came to accept that fact over time. Whenever their school doctor said or did something that left them scratching their heads, they'd dismiss it by saying, "That's just Doc Graham." One such instance came on a quiet summer afternoon when Graham noticed Frankie Centa getting a toy out of the penny gumball machine in front of the store his family owned. Graham watched intently as the youngster opened the prize. He then approached and offered to buy the round plastic container it came in for a quarter. "He said he needed it for an experiment," Centa recalled.

Another of Doc's idiosyncrasies was his penchant for chewing paper. "Healthier than tobacco," the fictional Graham remarks in *Shoeless Joe*. In reality, it was probably more a nervous habit than anything else. He'd pick up a spare sheet from his desk, bite off a corner, and begin chewing. After a few minutes, he'd spit the wad out, take another bite, and repeat the process. It was all relatively harmless, except on those occasions when Doc accidentally stuffed an important piece of paper into his mouth.

That happened to Jim Vitali and his friends once when they faked a pinkeye outbreak to get out of school early and play baseball. Graham, who probably knew what the boys were up to, wrote them excuses to explain their absences. But before handing them out, he balled them into tiny wads, jammed them into his mouth, chewed for a few seconds, and spit them into the waiting hands of aspiring pitchers, catchers, infielders, and outfielders. The youngsters had their written excuses, albeit a bit moist.

At least they were able to talk their way back into class the next day. John Tancabel wasn't as fortunate. A recent Chisholm High graduate, Tancabel returned one day to ask Graham for a letter of recommendation. Seconds after handing over the form that listed the prospective employer's address and phone number, he watched in shock as Graham instinctively crumpled it up and started chewing on it. "By the time he realized what he had done and handed it back, I couldn't read what was on the paper," Tancabel said. "All I could think was, 'There goes that job,' because I couldn't read the writing anymore and I couldn't remember the information that was on [the form]." He probably would have had just as much trouble reading the name and number if Doc had copied them for him. Graham's handwriting was so bad, even for a doctor, that his fellow Masons had to make him practice his signature three or four times before letting him sign their lodge's bylaws.

For all the respect and love he had for, and from, his patients, Graham was sometimes callous in his practice of medicine. This was particularly evident when he was called upon to perform the duties of eye doctor and audiologist.

Doc became famous for administering on-the-spot and unorthodox eye exams to squinting or red-eyed youngsters he ran into in the hallways. After peering into a student's eyes for a few seconds, he'd pull a pair of glasses from his pocket and, with the hastiest of instructions, hand it to the unsuspecting child. "Here's a pair of glasses," he'd say. "Take 'em with you."

When a youngster visited Graham at the unofficial office he set up in the old Rood Hospital across the street from his house, his procedures were no less startling. Before reaching into one of the countless crates of eyeglasses that filled the room, he would administer tests, demanding that his patients look through the doorways of two rooms to see eye charts. "It was kind of quaint," Bob McDonald recalled in 2005. Students would leave with a pair of "wire rims like the kids wear now," accompanied by quick and casual instructions for their use.

As might be expected, the unscientific process proved hit-or-miss. Another patient, Florene Luther, recalled feeling dizzy for the first few weeks after getting a pair of glasses from Doc Graham. Her mother, not knowing any better, told her to keep wearing them. "You'll get used to them," she said.

A few years later, Luther went to an eye doctor in Duluth to get her glasses adjusted while attending college there. It turned into a truly eye-opening experience.

"You got these from Dr. Graham of Chisholm? You're one of his patients?" the woman at the eyeglass company asked, horror in her voice. "It's a wonder you're not blind." Apparently, the prescription was nowhere near what it should have been.

"Now I know why I was dizzy the first few weeks I had the glasses," Luther said.

Nobody was ever quite certain where he got all the glasses he kept in his office, or how he paid for them, if he did at all. The crates just always seemed to be there, and they were never empty. For as long as anyone could remember, an endless supply of eyewear poured from the bottomless containers.

Graham was no less unconventional in his role as school audiologist. He started every new term by administering hearing tests to all the students of Chisholm. But because of the way he did it, no one ever failed. His secret to batting

Doc Graham fitting Jim Vitali with a pair of glasses. Later that year, Graham set Vitali up with a date for Chisholm High's junior prom.
COURTESY OF THE CHISHOLM HIGH *RANGER*

1.000 was well known among the students, who would wait in line outside Doc's office at the Washington School until it was their turn to be seen. One by one, he called the youngsters in and sat them down in a large wooden chair. Then he leaned in, put one hand up to his mouth, and whispered a number. The student repeated the number, and the test was over. The problem was that Graham employed the same number on every test and tended to raise his voice at times. He bellowed "Six!" so loudly one year that failure was impossible, recalled Ron Gornick, who grew up to become the executive director of the Chisholm Community Foundation. "Seven!" was heard all over Chisholm another year. Graham's number of choice varied from year to year but never during a given 12 months. It came at such ear-shattering volume that no recipient could fail to shout it back accurately.

Why no one ever objected to the way the hearing tests were administered is anybody's guess. It's impossible to know how many children went without having problems detected and treated. Likewise, few, if any, parents expressed concern about Graham's distribution of glasses, even though it violated one of the canons of his profession—namely, he dispensed prescriptions haphazardly or even recklessly. When pressed on the issue, most of his former patients had the same explanation: "That's just Doc Graham."

Though prone to flights of fancy, Graham was more than anything a creature of habit. He would wake before dawn each day and read the morning paper before heading off to school. He put his sock, shoe, and overshoe on his left foot before starting with the right because "the left is closest to the heart," according to nurse Frances Russ. He would put on the same hat and dark overcoat that flew behind him like a cape when he walked. He brought along an umbrella whether or not rain was in the forecast. On his way to work, he would stroll up and down the length of Lake Street, usually alone with his thoughts, stopping only to grab a donut and coffee at Pappas Bakery & Candy Kitchen. He was so obsessive about his routines that he would stop by Frank Tancabel's barbershop once a week to get a trim, even though he had more hair on his eyebrows than he did on top of his head.

"He had a little wart right next to his ear, and he'd say, 'Frank, don't cut that wart,' " Tancabel recalled years later, to which the barber would reply, "Doc, you don't even need a haircut."

"That's okay," Doc would say. "Cut it anyway."

Tancabel, who always humored his friend by going through the motions of giving him a haircut, concluded that the good doctor simply came in to socialize and thought he needed an excuse to be there.

Another of Graham's favorite pastimes was visiting his friend Andrew Niemalla, with whom he spent hours at a time allowing his imagination and long-suppressed ambition to run free. Publicly, he was an unlikely candidate to possess anything but pedestrian thoughts. Yet burning within the inner Doc was the unshakable conviction that celebrity would someday find him. In Chisholm, with the help of his partner Niemalla, he believed that feats of international importance lay just beyond his fingertips.

Niemalla, a tiny man who stood barely five-foot-five, was a mechanic and owner of the automobile garage on First Street. There, Doc worked on project after project in hopes of creating a contraption that would revolutionize the world. None of his experiments ever saw the light of day. But that never deterred him and his loyal assistant. "They wanted to hit the jackpot with an invention," recalled Vittori, a high-school student when he befriended Graham in 1930.

Graham's penchant for tinkering started innocently

enough. He began by taking spare wood from the lumber-
yard, attaching hinges, and making foldable yardsticks for
the teachers at school. He also made models of the heart and
used them to show schoolchildren how the organ worked.

Once Doc befriended Niemalla and gained access to the
mechanic's tool-filled shop, the projects became much more
sophisticated and ambitious. Outboard motors were outmod-
ed, they believed. The doctor and the mechanic concluded
that they could be replaced by inboard motors, which would
allow all boat parts to be free of the water. The idea, the pair
agreed, would revolutionize travel by water and simultane-
ously earn them riches and a place in the history of science.
But attempt after attempt always led them to the same dead
end. They were finally forced to conclude that, given the technology of the time, inboard motors were a dream.

Graham and Niemalla's other joint efforts ended with
similar disappointments. The doctor's decades-long attempts
to create a perpetual motion vehicle much like a Ferris wheel
produced only a string of failures. His vision centered around
a water-filled tank and a variety of tomato cans, their lids torn
off. It was Graham's belief that by reattaching the lids via sol-
dering, the empty cans could move smoothly and constantly
through the tank, which was several feet high and equally
long. Results, however, did not connect with theory. Despite
try after try, each preceded by weeks or months of rethinking,
reinvestigation, and readjustments of cans and tank, the bal-
ances and calibrations never produced the desired result.

Yet Graham and Niemalla never despaired. Like Walt
Whitman and his hopes for America, the M.D. and his side-
kick always looked to the future, confident that today's difficulties were but a prelude to tomorrow's successes.

Why Graham never made a breakthrough was puzzling
to some. "He was so brilliant," former assistant Mary Giannini

said. "That man thought he could invent anything." After his death, all that remained from his efforts were an odd assortment of paraphernalia tucked into the corners of the First Street garage and a room in his house filled nearly floor to ceiling with empty oatmeal boxes and tennis balls. "It was incredible," said Florene Luther, whose mother rented the apartment next door. "I think that was a part of that study he did with the blood pressure or some other kind of experiment."

The doctor and the mechanic began their unlikely friendship by accident. Graham was such a bad driver that he spent almost as much time getting his car worked on as he did driving it. At some point, he stopped being Niemalla's customer and became his friend.

Most of Graham's mishaps involved minor damage such as bent fenders, but he occasionally needed major repairs. Once, he went to Niemalla complaining that his bulky La-Salle had four flat tires. Doc was convinced that a group of local pranksters was responsible. But after getting the car up on jacks, Niemalla discovered that wasn't the case. "It seems that his throttle spring had broken off and the accelerator was stuck," said Gary Vukich, who befriended Graham while a student at Chisholm High. "He had driven all the way home from [the neighboring town of] Virginia riding his brakes, and the tubes literally melted."

Such instances and the fact that he could barely see over the big wooden steering wheel finally convinced Graham to hire somebody else to do the bulk of his driving for him. His chauffeurs were usually some of his favorite students from the local high school, a list that included Vittori, Vukich, Robert "Bogey" Dicklich, and Chisholm's future truant officer, John Zubitz. Their duties often forced them to sneak out of school to take Doc where he needed to go. Using a technique perfected by Vittori in the early 1930s, the driver would hide in the backseat of the sizable LaSalle (later replaced by an even bigger Cadillac) until Graham got it out of the parking lot. Once out of sight, Doc would switch places for the remainder of the trip. Most of the time, he paid his young assistant a few pennies for his efforts. On long trips, Graham would have his driver stop somewhere along the road so the two could enjoy an ice cream or other treat. Doc's favorite was a cup of hot coffee with a scoop of vanilla melting lusciously in it.

Twice a year, Graham would gather some of the boxes of eyeglasses he kept in his office and make the circuit selling them for six dollars apiece to people in Hibbing, Virginia, Duluth, and other nearby towns. Though the good doctor rarely opened up to his teenage associates during the long drives, Vittori said that his role allowed him to gain uncommon insight into a man who believed that his expertise and intellect could someday produce worldwide fame and mounds of money. But while Graham regularly engaged in strategies designed to earn great wealth, including owning numerous real-estate properties, he relished the pursuit of wealth much more than the actually possession of it.

This was best illustrated by the way he ran his rental properties in Chisholm and Hibbing, the neighboring city where, over the years, future celebrities including home-run king Roger Maris, basketball Hall of Famer Kevin McHale, and folk rock legend Bob Dylan were born or raised and where the Greyhound bus company was founded. Nobody is quite certain why Graham got involved in real estate. But once he did, he jumped in with both feet. "He bought up just about everything," newspaper publisher Veda Ponikvar said. That included the old Rood Hospital building across the street from his house. Doc set up a private office there and used the am-

Doc Graham has been honored by the citizens of the town he called "my most special place" with a billboard prominently displayed in downtown Chisholm.
Photo by Ron Gornick

bulance bay as a place to park his car while leasing out what was once the head doctor's quarters.

Rather than taking money for rent, Graham often bartered for goods and services ranging from landscaping and lawn care to fuel oil from a tenant who worked for the distributor. And he went for months or sometimes longer without cashing the checks of those who did pay him. "He would care less about the arrangement of things," longtime friend and Chisholm High basketball coach Bob McDonald said. "He just went about his business, and everything took care of itself. That was the beauty of him. That was the way he lived. Nothing ever seemed to bother him."

Not everyone thought Graham's relaxed business practices were so quaint. Money Kujala, who for 20 years lived with her family upstairs from Doc and Alecia, said she constantly complained to him about the upkeep of her apartment. "He certainly wasn't a good landlord," she said. "He never fixed anything. The back stairs were always falling apart, but he just didn't seem to be there all the time. It was like he was off in his own little world."

When repairs could no longer be avoided, Graham called his buddy Niemalla to make them. But that usually didn't work out well, since Niemalla was a mechanic, not a handyman trained in plumbing, carpentry, and electrical work. "He would just come over with a piece of string and fix the toilet with it for you," the daughter of another former tenant said. Some of Graham's properties grew so dilapidated that a half-block of buildings he owned on First Street was torn down shortly after his death in 1965.

Despite Graham's indifference toward maintenance, no one publicly confronted him about it. In most cases, the families to whom he rented were among the poorest in the region and were grateful to have roofs over their heads. Besides, he was the first to come to his tenants' aid when they went through difficult times. Once, when one of them was suddenly left a widow, Doc went out of his way to take the woman and her three children under his care, buying them gifts at Christmas, making sure food was always on their table, and paying at least one of the youngsters' way through college.

Another way he helped his poor tenants was by not cashing their rent checks. Then again, it's debatable whether his were acts of benevolence or just manifestations of his trademark absent-mindedness. Tancabel, the barber, told a story about a time when Graham didn't have enough cash in his pocket to pay for his weekly "haircut." Knowing that the doctor was good for it, Tancabel told him to pay the next time. But Graham was insistent. He pulled out his wallet and began rummaging through it to find a loose quarter or two. Instead, he came across what appeared to be about a dozen pieces of paper, each folded into a tiny square about the size of a postage stamp. Most were long-forgotten checks.

When the barber unfolded one and discovered that it was a government bond, his jaw dropped. "My God, Doc," he said. "You've got to cash this thing or put it away somewhere."

It was the kind of moment that led people in Chisholm to exclaim, "That's just Doc!" And it was hardly an isolated incident. "One thing that he did that used to aggravate everybody around was never bothering to cash their checks," McDonald, the basketball coach, said. "If you asked him what happened to one, he'd look through all his pockets, and there'd be 15 of them there. He'd have to look through them [to find the right one]. Most of the time, there's no telling where those things had gone."

If Doc had put all his remittances in the bank, rather than carrying them around until they got washed with his pants or lost, there's no telling how much money he would have had. The number of houses and buildings he owned was considerable. Among his properties was Edwardson's Bakery in Hibbing. As it was, he and Alecia had just enough to get by—and they gave much of that away to children on the street, local school teams, and anyone else who needed a handout. "He was a delightful, charming human being who was always broke," said Andy Shuster, Chisholm High class of 1940. Or as Graham's former assistant and tenant Giannini said, "He was real-estate rich, rent poor."

As caring and empathetic as Doc was, he could be just as brutally blunt, to a point that "would ordinarily offend people," according to Chisholm High swimming and baseball coach Bill Loushine. Graham was typically more sympathetic toward the youngsters for whom he cared than toward their parents, though he never pulled any punches. "He was very straightforward, very honest, direct," Veda Ponikvar said. "He told it like it was and didn't mince any words."

Such directness might not have gone over well back home in North Carolina, where gentlemen of Graham's stature were expected to comport themselves with politeness and gentility. It might have caused confrontation in a big city such as New York, where he completed most of his medical training. But in Chisholm, where he was loved and accepted for who he was, not who he was supposed to be, the quirky physician felt free to be himself without fear of repercussion.

The fictitious Doc in W. P. Kinsella's *Shoeless Joe* and the film adaptation *Field of Dreams* calls Chisholm "my most special place in all the world." And why not? Chisholm was where Graham could study the blood pressures of children without being called a quack, and where he could spend hour after hour on lazy afternoons with an uneducated auto mechanic searching for perpetual motion.

In the Walt Whitman tradition, a multitude of characteristics defined Doc Graham's reality. Maybe that's why all his attempts at invention led only to unrealized dreams. Graham's historic blood pressure study was inspired by the children he served and loved. But none of the machines he worked so diligently to create sprang from a similar source. Love of humankind propelled him to success; love of fame did not. Perhaps Doc Graham could touch the stars only when love directed his energies and talents.

CHAPTER 11

After School
A Public Servant to the End

> *"This is my most special place in all the world. Once a place touches you like that, the wind never blows so cold again."*
>
> MOONLIGHT GRAHAM IN THE
> NOVEL *SHOELESS JOE*

IN OCTOBER 1959, shortly after the school year began, Doc celebrated his 80th birthday. Though the occasion was marked by a small get-together among his friends and colleagues at the Washington School, the party was hardly joyous. Times were starting to get tough around the mines. More than 25 of them had shut down in the Iron Range during the preceding decade, and concerns had arisen that the Chisholm schools could no longer afford a staff doctor. Since his best friend and closest ally, J. P. Vaughan, had retired a few years earlier, Graham had started to hear whispers that he should do the same. But Doc had even more pressing concerns than keeping his job. His hearing and vision were faltering because of age, and that old respiratory condition that had led him to the Iron Range all those years earlier had begun to return. By the time school let out for the holidays that December, Doc decided he'd had enough. He announced his plans to retire at the end of the term in June 1960.

Retirement, however, didn't suit the old doctor well. He was far too fidgety and active to sit around watching Alecia and her friends play cards or to hang around the house doing nothing. Even with all his rental properties and a scaled-down private practice, he still needed an outlet to help keep him busy and to help him stop feeling so detached from the young people he'd been around for nearly a half-century.

He finally found it in the spring of 1962 after a friend suggested he run for a spot on the Chisholm School Board in the upcoming election. Back in the 1930s, Doc had served a term on the city council and had been among those who approved the plan to build the Bridge of Peace across Longyear Lake. A few years later, he made an unsuccessful bid to become mayor. Still, he was hardly a politician with expertise in such matters as budgets, contracts, and *Robert's Rules of Order*. But he had nothing better to do. Besides, everyone in town already knew and respected him, so why not? What he lacked in campaign savvy he made up for in personality and a natural ability to connect with his constituency.

Using the slogan "Your Children Are Your Greatest Asset," and running on the experience gained from 44 years in the schools, Graham was one of four candidates to advance through the primary. He received 556 votes of the 1,955 ballots cast, placing him fourth behind incumbent Edward LaFrance, Eugene "Jim" Belluzzo, and Bob Vukad. Two open seats were to be filled.

The general election was held May 14, 1962. The popular

After retiring as Chisholm's school doctor, Graham found another way to help the town's children by running for the school board. Although he lost the election of 1962, during which he used this campaign poster, he won a seat a year later.
COURTESY OF THE LYNN WIL-LIAMSON DIDIER COLLECTION

doctor, running on a platform that stressed his beliefs "in keeping mathematics, physics and Latin in our schools" and in helping parents keep their children in school "to avoid later regrets," had his work cut out for him. All three of his foes had children in the Chisholm schools, all were World War II veterans, and all were employed by a local mining company. LaFrance, who like Graham had played minor league baseball, was already a board member. Vukad had a public-service résumé that included two terms as a city alderman and one on the Chisholm Police Commission. He was the chairman of the joint city-county recreation board at the time of the election.

Doc never had a chance, finishing third behind LaFrance and Belluzzo. But instead of being discouraged, he came away invigorated after garnering 1,065 votes. His surprisingly strong showing inspired him to plan another run the following year, when two more seats would come open.

In early April 1963, on the first day candidates were allowed to file, he rushed to the courthouse, paid his fee, and got his name back on the ballot. Again, he won enough support in the primary to make it through to the general election on May 27. This time, he faced an even more difficult race, against not one but two incumbent opponents—Charles Prebil and Paul Perkovich. This time, though, Graham's lack of political experience might actually have worked to his advantage.

Times were changing on the Iron Range, and not necessarily for the better. Both mineral values and the population of the area were declining as the last remaining veins of high-grade ore were extracted from the ground in the aftermath of World War II. As mining companies began looking elsewhere for the precious iron and the jobs it brought, enrollment in Chisholm's once-thriving schools took a nosedive. By the spring of 1963, fewer than 2,000 children remained in grades K-12. With fewer students came fewer tax dollars from the state of Minnesota, creating a huge budget deficit that forced the school board to cut back on everything from teacher raises to hot lunches in the high school. Among the ideas to help save money was a proposal that board members give up their $250 monthly salary and work for free. "Many people feel it is the duty of the civic-minded citizen to serve the school board without pay," the *Chisholm Free Press* suggested.

In that same issue about two weeks before the general election, the newspaper's editors asked each of the four candidates their opinions on that and several other subjects. Prebil and Perkovich, the two sitting members, were adamant about keeping their modest paychecks. "In order to be properly informed in making decisions, a [board] member has the loss of working hours and income and I feel that some sort of compensation should be received," Prebil said. "Because of my time of being on the board, I have actually lost money serving the people of our community," Perkovich echoed.

Graham took the opposite view. Never mind that he was retired and had plenty of time on his hands, or that money had never been high on his list of priorities. His answer immediately endeared him to an electorate desperate for leaders to help get them through difficult financial times. "In my opinion," the good doctor said, "the [school] directors are overpaid." He also derided the current board for spending several thousand dollars on hiring consultants to assess the school system's needs. Those experts, brought in from the University of Minnesota in Minneapolis, had recommended that several new classrooms and a new boiler be added to the Lincoln school. The plan had been implemented in 1960, but within three years, those new classrooms—along with several others in Chisholm Junior High and Vaughan-Steffensrud Elementary—were sitting unused. Graham blamed the situation on outsiders "spending other people's money and running us farther into debt."

Apparently, Doc's financial conservatism struck a chord with the usually liberal voters of Chisholm. When the ballots were counted and the election results were announced that Tuesday night in May 1963, both incumbents had been unseated. John Dwyer, Jr., a local businessman and member of the town's library board, received 1,287 votes. Right behind him was everybody's favorite ballplayer, doctor, friend, and philanthropist, Dr. A. W. Graham, with 1,233. He edged Prebil by six votes to earn the second and final three-year term. The result was so close that the 10 spoiled ballots disqualified by election officials could easily have swung the results. But it didn't matter. Doc had won and for the first time since his retirement, he was again officially working for the betterment of the children he had spent his life loving and protecting.

The task began right away. As Graham quickly discovered, the maladies afflicting Chisholm's school system would take more than just a swab of Mercurochrome.

One of the first major issues that confronted him and his fellow board members was teacher pay. Following a call to the Minnesota Department of Education for help in financing the plan, Superintendent Eugene Eininger recommended that $20,000 be allocated for raises across the board. That might have sounded like a lot of money during that era, but in reality, a second-year teacher with a bachelor's degree would see only about $150 more per year, going from $5,300 to $5,450. A teacher with a master's degree would see a raise from $6,800 annually to $7,000. Nevertheless, two board members—Dwyer and William Olsen—voted against the plan. Graham sided with the three others and helped it pass. That soon became a pattern.

"I remember him sitting at the meetings, all dressed up

with the suit and tie—the works," said fellow board member Jim Vitali. "He really didn't want to get into anything divisive. He was like, 'I'll be here, but if something controversial comes up, I might have to see a patient or something like that.' " Because he was reluctant to ruffle feathers, Graham almost always voted with the majority, regardless of the issue. When it appeared that his might not be the popular opinion, he quickly changed sides in the middle of a debate.

An example came on April 23, 1964, when Dwyer recommended that the board publicly endorse the controversial "Taconite Amendment" being debated in the state legislature. Taconite, the small, high-grade pellets of iron ore that still blanketed the red hills of the range, was looked upon as the region's saving grace because of its growing popularity as blast furnace feed. But because the mining companies were reluctant to spend the money needed to change their existing operations over to the new technology, they simply moved elsewhere to start over from scratch. In an effort to keep the companies in Minnesota—and, specifically, the Iron Range—politicians decided to offer a 25-year exemption on tax increases for any taconite plant built in the state. The amendment was to be decided by the voters in November. Its passage was considered essential for the survival of Chisholm's economy. Doc Graham had said as much in his campaign a year earlier: "If the Taconite Amendment does not pass, the Range will be on the road to yesterday." Then, noting that the legislature had already turned down one opportunity to let the people vote on the bill, he had quoted Shakespeare: " 'What fools these mortals be.' "

Unfortunately, his convictions weren't as strong as his rhetoric. When fellow member Edward LaFrance expressed concern about the board's taking a stand on the Taconite Amendment, suggesting instead that it wait until people had time to weigh both sides of the matter, Graham immediately withdrew his support of Dwyer's motion.

The issue wasn't going away. In September, enrollment in the Chisholm schools decreased further. When Superintendent Eininger submitted a $1.314 million budget for the 1964–65 school year, the debate began to heat up again. In the meantime, Eininger informed the school board that more cuts would have to be made. He then fired off an impassioned letter to Governor Karl Rolvaag pleading for help. The basis of his argument was that Chisholm had one of the richest systems in Minnesota based on mineral valuations, but because of the per capita system used to determine financial aid, it actually was among the state's poorest. The situation had everyone at their wit's end. "If I seem upset," Eininger wrote to Rolvaag, "I am."

The collective attitude improved considerably on the morning of November 5, 1964, and not just because Minnesota's favorite son, Senator Hubert H. Humphrey, was elected in a landslide to become Lyndon B. Johnson's vice president. "In unprecedented numbers and with unbelievable enthusiasm," the *Chisholm Tribune-Press* reported, "voters turned out Tuesday and served notice that they are willing to assure to mining investors that their taxes will not be increased disproportionately for the next 25 years." On the same day that the Taconite Amendment was adopted, two companies—Hanna Mining and U.S. Steel—announced plans to open new plants, bringing more than 4,000 jobs and an estimated $50 million in income to Chisholm and the surrounding area. The welcome news allowed Graham to feel much more secure about the future of his beloved home, even though he knew it was a future he wouldn't live to see.

His declining health was now evident as early as 1959, when for the second time in eight years the Chisholm

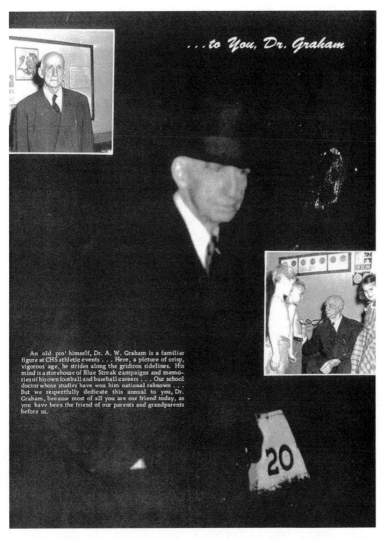

...to You, Dr. Graham

An old pro' himself, Dr. A. W. Graham is a familiar figure at CHS athletic events . . . Here, a picture of crisp, vigorous age, he strides along the gridiron sidelines. His mind is a storehouse of Blue Streak campaigns and memories of his own football and baseball careers . . . Our school doctor whose studies have won him national reknown . . . But we respectfully dedicate this annual to you, Dr. Graham, because most of all you are our friend today, as you have been the friend of our parents and grandparents before us.

Doc Graham was among the first to practice what is now known as sports medicine. His reassuring presence on the sidelines at Chisholm High Blue Streaks athletic events earned him the admiration of his students, who dedicated their 1959 school annual in his honor.
COURTESY OF THE CHISHOLM HIGH *RANGER*

High yearbook, *The Ranger*, was dedicated to him. Though the text waxed poetic about his "crisp, vigorous . . . strides along the athletic sidelines," the accompanying pictures told a different story. Graham looked drawn, tired, and hunched in his trademark black trench coat and wide-brimmed hat. His once-pronounced black eyebrows had turned a much less noticeable white, and his hair was gone. Over time, his morning walks had become shorter and shorter, and he often had to stop to catch his breath. At the monthly school board meetings, it wasn't unusual for him to fall asleep in his chair if the discussion got too lengthy or the subject matter didn't interest him.

Then there was the issue of his memory, especially where it pertained to his long-ago professional baseball career. Doc had always shied away from talking about the subject except in the most ambiguous terms. But now, in his old age, he began to volunteer information to whoever would listen. The problem was that not all his facts were accurate. Whether he made a conscious attempt at deception or his memories had become blurred by time, Graham had a tendency to overstate his diamond accomplishments in his later years. He told the *Duluth News-Tribune*, for instance, that he had led the Eastern League in hitting in 1903, when in fact his average was just .240 for Nashua and Manchester of the New England League.

But that was nothing compared to what he told the *Charlotte News* on July 17, 1963. In an interview during what would be the old doctor's final trip to his old home, he told a young reporter named Ernie Accorsi that he hit 53 points higher than he actually had for the Charlotte Hornets of 1902. He followed that up by telling the biggest whopper of all—that he actually got a chance to bat in the major leagues. According to Accorsi's story, Graham claimed to have walked in his only plate appearance before suffering a career-ending broken leg while attempting to steal second. It was only years later, after he saw *Field of Dreams*, that Accorsi realized he'd been had. "He didn't come off as a man whose mind was wandering," said the former reporter, who went on to become general manager of the National Football League's Baltimore Colts, Cleveland Browns, and New York Giants. "He remembered so many things and had so many recollections. For whatever reason, he just decided to embellish things a little." In retrospect, Accorsi said that it was almost as if Graham had been "reading a cue card" while describing his accomplishments.

Yet even though his grasp of the truth had apparently escaped him, Doc still had an amazing knack for conjuring up a little magic from the moonlight. On the night he returned to the ballpark to commemorate his old team's record 25-game winning streak, the Hornets were inspired to win for the first time after 13 consecutive losses.

Back home in Minnesota, Graham found himself spending an increasing amount of time with another member of the media. At first, he started hanging out with Veda Ponikvar because the office of the *Chisholm Free Press* and *Tribune-Press* was located about halfway up Lake Street, and he no longer had the energy to walk any farther. He also came to like and respect the spitfire of an editor and publisher whose aggressive style and biting opinions made her famous as far away as Washington, D.C. Despite their difference in age, Doc felt comfortable with Veda. Rather than telling her tall tales about his baseball glory, he spoke of events from Chisholm's past— rebuilding from the great fire of 1908, the typhoid epidemic of 1910, the Depression. Their conversations became an unofficial oral town history. One morning, Graham brought a present with him. It was a yellowing picture of a grim-faced baseball player, cap cocked to the left, determined look in his eyes, the letters N and Y emblazoned across his chest. The wallet-sized photo was Doc's only memento of his brief stay in the major leagues. And now he was handing it over to the local newspaper publisher as something of a last will and testament to the people and town he loved so dearly.

Doc knew he was declining fast. But that didn't stop his fellow members of the Chisholm School Board from appointing him their treasurer on July 8, 1965. He tried to tell them he wasn't up to the job. They didn't listen. Apparently, the other board members were less interested in being practical than in honoring him for nearly a half-century of public service.

They might have thought differently had they consulted with Graham's next-door neighbor Mary Giannini, who sensed something was wrong after running into her landlord one afternoon in early August.

"What's the matter, Doc?" she asked.

"I got something right here in my lungs," he replied. "I'm not going to last."

Graham was true to his word. That was the last time Giannini saw him alive.

"He didn't say anything to anybody that he was sick," she recalled years later. "He just knew he was going."

Doc lasted long enough to attend one more school board meeting, on August 11. That night, he voted with the majority—as usual—in approving a $780 per month allocation to the Chisholm Transportation Company for the use of two school buses. Once the final vote was taken, Graham shook a few hands, put on his hat and overcoat, said goodbye, and headed home. He checked into the hospital not long afterward. On Wednesday, August 25, the man described in the *Free Press* as "one of Chisholm's most revered pioneers and a favorite of every student" died.

"One night, he just died in his sleep," his friend Veda recalled. A few days later, she wrote and published an editorial entitled, "His Was a Life of Greatness":

The greatness of any community can be measured by the contributions of its citizenry along the journey of life.

For Chisholm an era of rich and purposeful living slipped into another shadow of twilight with the passing of the beloved and deeply respected Dr. Archibald Graham. Early in life, Doc chose to be a very unusual man. With the Blueridge mountains at his feet; the peach orchards in his back yard and the warmth and gentility of the South a distinct part of his upbringing, he could have chosen the easy, lazy, uneventful path of existence.

His father was a successful and accomplished attorney. His mother the epitome of Southern grace and charm. Their influence led Doc to seek his Bachelor's degree and then his Doctor of Medicine in an era when education was the exception rather than the accepted mode of life.

A deep thinker and scholar, Dr. Graham was interested in research and spent days, weeks and months studying, diagnosing, testing. And just as he whetted and challenged his mind to probe for the knowledge that would help to save lives in later generations, so he disciplined and trained his body to remain sound and energetic. He was a great athlete, disciplining himself to a rigid schedule of exercise and body training. To play with the New York Giants while still going to college was no small feat, but Doc had that kind of perseverance and that kind of stamina.

Following his internship in the great hospitals and medical centers in the east, this healer of men could have commanded the highest paid positions in the largest and most advanced hospitals of the great metropolitan centers. Instead, he chose to come to a new, growing community of lumberjacks, miners and toiling farmers. His Rood Hospital was a landmark for a number of years in the heart of Chisholm, and with his practice, his circle of friends and associates expanded in every direction. He was a kindly, understanding humanitarian physician. Never did he ask for money or fees; but he always gave of himself. Every summer, for many years, he would take vacation and return to the great medical centers in the east to probe and study further. What he learned he brought back and applied the new knowledge in his practice.

Doc's capabilities did not go un-noticed, and before too many years passed, the late Superintendent J. P. Vaughan persuaded this still young, highly skilled doctor to join the school medical staff. Then began a career of testing young children for heart and blood pressure abnormalities that has met no equal. Medical records and journals have recorded for all time the magnificent work of Chisholm's Doc Graham. His follow-up programs in the field over the many years became recognized by the medics of the nation. This was indeed a unique and most revealing program.

As the community grew, Doc became an integral part of the population. There were good years and lean ones. There were times when children could not afford eye glasses or milk or clothing because of the economic upheavals, strikes and depressions. Yet no child was ever denied these essentials, because in the background, there was a benevolent, under-standing Doctor Graham. Without a word, without any fan-fare or publicity, the glasses or the milk, or the ticket to the ball game found their way into the child's pocket.

As the years slipped by, and there were over forty of them of faithful and uninterrupted service, Doc became a legend. He was the champion of the oppressed; the grand marshal of every football, basketball and baseball game. He encouraged youth to train and play; he always carried that extra candy bar for the energy some lanky, hungry lad needed; and he was the first one at the side of the boy who got hurt in any sport. Doc was just that kind of a man. And when it came to support of civic projects, Doc was the first to buy tickets and lend his support. He believed in the community and the parents and children believed in him.

There were many simple humble things that made Doc happy, but his eyes beamed brightest like a galaxy of stars whenever he read or heard of a student from Chisholm who had done well . . . who had gone forth to achieve . . . who reached the apex of perfection in his chosen endeavor. He remembered everybody by name and in his travels, took signal pride in telling everybody about a town called Chisholm and its cradle of many tongues and creeds.

For the old and young of this little mining town who knew Doctor Graham . . . his era was a historic, unique sort of legend. There will never be another quite like it.

Ponikvar's heartfelt testimonial wasn't entirely accurate. Graham was born in Fayetteville and grew up in Charlotte, neither of which placed "the Blueridge mountains at his feet." And while his father had attended law school at Columbia, he made his name as an educator, not as "a successful and accomplished attorney."

Nonetheless, the tribute became a well-known piece of journalism—first because it was entered into the *Congressional Record* by Vice President Humphrey and Representative John A. Blatnik on September 17, 1965, then 20 years later when excerpts were included in the script of *Field of Dreams.* It was also the first of many tributes to a man Blatnik, a Chisholm native, said "personified humility and practiced a truly edifying love of his fellow man." Among the most personal was the Dr. A. W. Graham Memorial Fund, started by a group of friends shortly after Doc's death. The fund raised thousands of dollars for the Range Day Care Center for the Mentally Retarded.

When it came time to say goodbye, virtually the entire community turned out. According to Ponikvar, the line outside the Rupp Funeral Home for Doc's viewing was "absolutely endless." Unfortunately, Frank Graham didn't arrive from North Carolina in time to witness the outpouring of love and respect. All he saw was a half-empty sanctuary at Chisholm's Community Methodist Church for the funeral, and he wasn't

Newspaper publisher Veda Ponikvar is shown here dedicating a memorial to Chisholm residents killed in foreign wars. She is flanked by Paul Marturano (left) and Major General D. E. Larson of the United States Air Force. Veda was one of Doc Graham's best friends. Thanks to the movie Field of Dreams, *she has become something of a celebrity in her own right.*
COURTESY OF THE CITY OF CHISHOLM, MINNESOTA

happy about it. "You'd think that the whole town would come out because he helped the kids so much," the former United States senator told Mary Giannini. "But nobody came to do anything for him."

Frank knew better than that. He just wasn't thinking clearly after the long trip to Minnesota and after realizing that the big brother he had always idolized was gone. His anger turned to compassion when he saw how badly his sister-in-law needed him in her time of loss. Docky was more than just a husband to Alecia. He was her provider, her constant companion, her entire world. They had been married one month shy of 50 years, and when he was taken away from her, it was as if a piece of her died, too. He had loved her just as much. Before he left, Doc had overwhelmed Alecia with one last token far more meaningful than any of the blue hats he never got around to giving her. He agreed to be buried in Rochester—in a Catholic cemetery, no less.

Exactly how Alecia was able to convince the people at Calvary Cemetery to allow Doc, a Presbyterian who had refused to convert even in his dying days, to be interred in consecrated ground isn't certain. Father Murphy, the hot-blooded priest who married the Grahams at St. John's Church, would have been horrified. And yet she pulled it off. Her small victory provided only momentary consolation from her grief, though. Doc's death left a void in her heart nothing could possibly fill. Frank did what he could to comfort her. So did Alecia's sisters once she arrived in Rochester for the burial. They tried to convince her to stay, but even though it meant leaving her beloved husband behind, she insisted on returning to Chisholm. She even agreed to serve out the final year of Doc's term on the school board.

It turned out to be a bad decision. As strong and independent as Alecia was in her younger days, she had grown accustomed to having someone around to take care of her. Living alone represented a major change. She didn't adapt to it well. She attended only one or two school board meetings, if that many, and was rarely seen outside her house or yard. Her friends and neighbors began to whisper that she was suffering from dementia. That diagnosis was reinforced one afternoon when Giannini found Alecia lying on the basement floor of the Grahams' apartments. It appeared that she had fallen down the stairs.

"Mary, you haven't paid your light bill," she said.

"Alecia, are you okay?" Giannini asked.

"Mary, you haven't paid your light bill," Alecia repeated.

"But Alecia, I pay my own bill and you pay yours," Giannini replied.

No matter how hard Giannini tried to convince her landlord that the bill wasn't her responsibility, Alecia wouldn't listen. What's worse, Alecia seemed dazed and out of touch with reality. So after helping the frail old woman up the stairs, Giannini called a doctor. Next, she got in touch with Alecia's sister Grace, who arrived the following weekend with family members to clean out the house and move Alecia to a nursing home in Winona. She lived there for 15 years until 1981, when at the age of 95 she died of complications from a stroke. She was buried next to Doc in Calvary Cemetery, right across the street from St. John's. A few paces away, under a sprawling shade tree, were the graves of her cousin J. P. and her best friend, Leathe Vaughan.

Doc and Alecia were a long way from Chisholm, where they met, thrived, and helped enrich the lives of virtually everyone they touched. But at least they were back together again.

CHAPTER 12

Fact, Film, and Fantasy

"Go the distance!"
THE VOICE FROM THE MOVIE
FIELD OF DREAMS

THE MEMORY BEGINS TO PLAY TRICKS as the days and months fade into years and decades. Details become confused. Faces turn fuzzy. Facts turn into romanticized fiction.

On this much, everyone agrees: It was unseasonably hot in Chisholm, Minnesota, on the early-summer afternoon that would ultimately turn Dr. Archibald W. Graham immortal. It was so sweaty and uncomfortable on June 3, 1980, that Veda Ponikvar decided to send everyone home early from the tiny Lake Street office of the biweekly local newspaper she published. Ponikvar, a dynamic little woman who rubbed elbows with powerful politicians such as Vice President Walter Mondale and continued to work with NORAD long after she was discharged from the military, was about to head home herself when the visitors arrived unannounced.

The way she remembers it, the two men pulled up in a black rumble seat Ford and walked through the door wearing black suits that made them look like the Blues Brothers. Their appearance was so sinister that she thought she was about to be robbed. "I remember grabbing the cashbox and trying to hide it," she recalled more than 30 years later. But the men weren't interested in money. They came looking for information—specifically, as many facts as they could unearth about a certain old ballplayer whose major league career lasted but an instant a lifetime ago.

"Oh, you mean Doc Graham," Ponikvar remembers saying.

"No, I believe his name was Moonlight," one of the men replied.

"That's him," Ponikvar said. "His baseball career didn't amount to much, so he went to school and became a doctor."

The scene was chronicled by author W. P. Kinsella in the novel *Shoeless Joe*, then adapted for the hit movie *Field of Dreams*. To this day, Ponikvar swears that the man accompanying Kinsella that stiflingly hot June day was none other than reclusive author J. D. Salinger. It lives on in her memory as if it happened yesterday, even if the details of the encounter aren't quite the same as how Kinsella remembers them.

As he recalls, he was driving an old mustard-colored Datsun when he rolled into town looking to attach a personality to a colorful nickname and a single line of type from the *Baseball Encyclopedia*. Instead of a black suit, he recalls wearing shorts, a cheesy Hawaiian shirt, and his trademark cowboy hat. And that partner? In Kinsella's fictionalized version in *Shoeless Joe*, it is indeed Salinger. But in real life, it was Kinsella's wife, Ann. It seems Ponikvar is conflating the two.

"Veda, she sincerely believes what she's telling you," Kinsella says. "She's told the story over and over again so many times that to her, it's become fact. But I've never met J. D. Salinger."

Chisholm has no greater benefactor than Ponikvar, who over the decades has met with and hosted dozens of nationally and internationally known figures. As late as 2004, she was responsible for bringing Democratic presidential nominee John Kerry to Chisholm, no small feat considering the size of the town and the significance of the office. So if she changed a few facts to glamorize her story, it was with Chisholm's best interests at heart. She can be excused for her confusion, because when it comes to the details of Graham's life, everyone seems to want to "swirl the ingredients together," as Kinsella once noted, "into an exotic cocktail of fact, fiction and fantasy."

Even his birth date is disputed. Most baseball records, including those in the *Baseball Encyclopedia* and the Baseball Hall of Fame in Cooperstown, New York, list Graham as having been born on November 9, 1876. That same year is even chiseled into the granite of his headstone. Where it came from is uncertain, but it's almost certainly wrong. Though the state of North Carolina did not issue official birth certificates until early in the 20th century, several reliable documents—including United States Census forms, University of North Carolina and University of Maryland alumni records, and a petition to become a Mason, written and signed in Graham's own handwriting—list the actual date as November 10, 1879.

That mystery is part of what makes him such a fascinating figure. The other half of the equation is that there is no way to prove or disprove many of the myths that surround him. Because he was an obscure country doctor to all but those in his small sphere of influence, no one thought to save any of his papers or records. They were either thrown away at the time

Visitors to Graham's grave site regularly leave baseballs, candy, and coins so he'll always have something to throw to the children he loved so much. But a quick check of this headstone shows a mistake in his date of birth.

NATIONAL BASEBALL HALL of FAME and MUSEUM, INC.

Cooperstown, New York

March 27, 1960

Dr. Archibald W. Graham,
Chisholm, Minnesota.

Dear Dr.Graham:

It was very kind of you to return your questionnaire to us by registered mail, but I'm sorry you went to that expense. At any rate, we are very happy to have your address and data.

Mrs. John J. McGraw still comes up here every summer, and I believe that this year she is going to be at the opening game at San Francisco.

I wonder if you would be kind enough to complete your questionnaire by giving us the exact date in 1915 - month and date that you were married. When we have this information, our record on you will be complete.

Enclosed is a ⸺⸺⸺⸺ed envelope. No postage will be necessary.

With thanks

Sincerely,

Lee Allen

Lee Allen,
Historian

Letter sent to Doc by the Hall of Fame asking for updated information for its records
COURTESY OF THE LYNN WILLIAMSON DIDIER COLLECTION

of his death or destroyed when the Washington School was later demolished.

About the only way to identify the whole truth of Graham's life story is to stroll the streets of Chisholm after dark, hoping to run into his ghost the way the fictional Ray Kinsella does in *Field of Dreams*. But even that might not be fruitful, since the Chisholm that appears on film isn't actually Chisholm. It's not even Minnesota. Rather, it's Galena, Illinois, a small town selected as a stand-in because of its proximity to the main filming location in Iowa. It's one of the many inaccuracies W. P. Kinsella likes to call "creative nonfiction" that are included in the movie and the book that inspired it.

Among the most glaring is the timing of Graham's short stay in the major leagues. On film, the young Moonlight's one moment in the sun comes on the final day of the regular season, and he retires immediately thereafter because he "couldn't bear the thought of another year in the minors." In fact, his "two joyous innings in the right garden" for John McGraw's New York Giants came at midseason, on Thursday, June 29. And he continued to harbor dreams of getting back to the big time for nearly a decade after being shipped to Scranton of the New York State League.

In fiction, Doc plays for the Giants in 1922, rather than 1905; bats right handed instead of left handed; and was born in Minnesota, not North Carolina. His father is portrayed by Hollywood as a doctor, not a respected educator. And because the real-life Graham worked for the school system and wasn't in private practice, his office was in the Washington School, not downtown Chisholm, as in the movie.

These are all flaws Graham would have noticed and grumbled about, had he lived long enough to see himself on the big screen. But other than that, those who knew him best believe he would have been happy with the way he is portrayed in

Field of Dreams—especially that he finally gets to take a swing at a major league pitcher. "I think he would have relished that in a way, not from the standpoint of an immodest type of behavior, but because of the fulfillment of the dream of the trail he was supposed to lead," says longtime Chisholm High basketball coach Bob McDonald. "He never talked about what he had done. He was a modest fellow. It all came out after he'd passed away."

As for memories of Graham, everyone in Chisholm born before 1960 has at least one. For Veda Ponikvar, it's those lazy afternoons with Doc in the newspaper office, talking about the past. For Angelo Vittori, it's the sight of the old doctor and his auto mechanic friend, Andrew Niemalla, trying to create perpetual motion. For Jim Vitali, it's an unforgettable prom night made possible by a kindly father figure.

Other memories aren't verifiable. The most sensational is from the mid-1920s, when the great Shoeless Joe Jackson is said to have appeared on the Iron Range to play a little baseball. Jackson had been banned from the game by then because of his participation in the 1919 Chicago "Black Sox" scandal. But in order to continue earning a paycheck, he barnstormed around the country, playing wherever he could. Most of the time, he appeared under an assumed name to avoid attention. That was the case the day he rolled into Chisholm for a game against the local team, known as the Flyers, and a certain right fielder who would one day become linked with Jackson in literature and legend. An account of that meeting between the two old kids from the Carolinas appears on the back of a commemorative baseball card produced by Mike Kalibabky in 1999. The account is based on stories told by those who were there.

The game was played at the edge of Pig Town in the old ballpark bordering on the local iron ore mine. Author Jerry

Sonosky wrote that "if you went after a long fly ball and mis-judged the distance to the pit, you'd go flyin' and tumblin' right in." According to Sonosky, Chisholm led the visitors by three runs in the bottom of the ninth when, with two outs and the bases loaded, the man purported to be Shoeless Joe came to the plate. Jackson then hit one "a mile high and deep, but not deep enough so that Moonlight couldn't make a spectacular one-handed catch before falling backwards into the pit, still clutching the ball for a clean out."

Twenty years later, Graham met up with another great left-hand-hitting outfielder. Only this time, the story wasn't quite as dramatic and many more witnesses were present.

Hall of Famer Ted Williams made several trips to Chisholm early in his career with the Boston Red Sox. A passionate outdoorsman, he learned of the great hunting and fishing in the Minnesota wilderness during minor league stops in Minneapolis in 1937 and 1938. At that time, Williams befriended many locals, including Chisholm hotel owner Oscar Dornack. The enigmatic slugger hated people who put on airs almost as much as he despised the media circus that surrounded him wherever he went in Boston. Even after hitting the big time with the Red Sox, he valued the Iron Range as a place where he could escape the spotlight and enjoy some precious free time in relative anonymity with people who weren't awed by his celebrity. The fact that the lakes surrounding Chisholm were filled with walleye didn't hurt either.

Williams spent countless hours at Dornack's home when the two weren't hunting or fishing. According to Dornack's daughter Joanne, her father was fond of taking Williams to the local hospitals to tour the children's wards. It was on one of those visits that the Splendid Splinter ran into Moonlight Graham. The two also met many times at Dornack's Tibroc Hotel during the Thursday-night smorgasbord, which was so popular that the line stretched around the post office and down to the Rupp Funeral Home, two blocks away on Third Avenue. Though numerous accounts of their face-to-face encounters exist, no one is sure what they talked about.

Their personalities were as different as the rival Red Sox and Yankees. Williams loved the great outdoors and hated ties. Graham rarely ventured from his home when he wasn't working and always dressed up, no matter what the occasion. Williams liked to have a good time with the local bar crowd and was a notorious ladies' man who was married three times, while Graham was devoted to his one true love, Alecia. The one thing they had in common was hitting. And since they were described by mutual friend Ray Maturi as being "polite, friendly, and nice" toward each other, that may have been what they spent their time together discussing.

One baseball event Graham studiously avoided was his short time with the Giants. It was a subject he rarely, if ever, discussed with anyone outside his tightest circle of family and friends. "Many of the people in Chisholm didn't even know he played ball at that level," W. P. Kinsella says. "He could have been one of those American Legion drunks who spent the next 70 years telling everybody, 'Yeah, I played for the New York Giants.' But Doc never mentioned it at all."

That began to change later in his life. Perhaps haunted by the long-suppressed regret of having come so close to realizing his dream, Graham concocted a plausibly fictitious story that expanded his role in "the bigs." There's no telling how many times he recited the tall tale that allowed him to fulfill his wish of holding a bat and running the bases in a major league game. Graham didn't seem to mind when the story was printed as fact in the *Charlotte News* on July 18, 1963. A walk, after all, does not count as an official at-bat, so his statistics in the *Baseball Encyclopedia* would remain unchallenged.

Because he never dreamed he would become as famous as he did after his death, he probably assumed no one would care enough to take the time to check the records and contradict his claim.

But W. P. Kinsella did. In doing so, he stumbled upon a story so unique and inspiring that the name Moonlight Graham has become a symbol for faith, forgiveness, and second chances. Those ideals continue to inspire nearly a half-century after his death and more than 20 years after he was introduced to millions in *Field of Dreams*.

Chisholm resident Mike Kalibabky was so inspired that he began a charitable foundation in Graham's name to provide scholarship money to the children the good doctor loved so much. Through the sale of $1 commemorative baseball cards he designed and produced himself, Kalibabky has raised more than $20,000 since 1993. "For some reason, people are compelled about his story because of the movie," he says. "I can always tell when *Field of Dreams* is replayed on cable, because the card sales usually spike. It's amazing. I've had orders from as far away as England and Japan. People can't believe he was a real person."

When they do find out, they can't seem to get enough. Graham's character has become such a marketable commodity that in 2000, a self-proclaimed baseball nut named Bart Silberman decided to name his nostalgic line of baseball-themed apparel after the world's most famous one-game wonder. He did it because old-timers such as Graham "bring us back to the romance of the sport, a better time and place." In keeping with that belief, Silberman's company donates a portion of its profits each year to the Doc Graham Scholarship Fund.

Around that same time, Ohio musicians Chris Bailey and Bill Littleford took on the name Moonlight Graham for their country folk band. "I had always been a fan of Archie Graham ever since being introduced to him in *Field of Dreams*," Bailey says. "I was intrigued by his story. It has a real follow-your-dreams sort of message everyone in American can relate to."

But the good doctor's fame isn't restricted to his home country. His appeal is so widespread that in 2003, Japanese producer Cyg Mori sent a five-member crew all the way to Minnesota to research and film a documentary on the *Field of Dreams* icon. The 50-minute production, which also has a segment on Shoeless Joe Jackson, was aired for a national audience in Japan by the NHK network on the *Sports Fans Club* television program. Among the dramatizations Mori's crew filmed were scenes depicting Graham's 1909 arrival in Chisholm, his coaching a group of children at the local ball field, and a dreamlike conversation between him and Jackson on the porch of Graham's house.

In a way, the Japanese film crew, baseball card collectors, and all those fans who listen to the music or wear the clothes bearing Doc's name have a lot in common with the children who were once drawn to him in hopes that he might toss some candy or coins in their direction. Graham's Pied Piper quality continues to draw people in.

On June 29, 2005, a crowd of 24,546 gathered at the Hubert H. Humphrey Metrodome in Minneapolis to celebrate the 100th anniversary of Graham's one game in the majors. Among the fans was a group of several hundred Chisholm residents. The Minnesota Twins hosted the Kansas City Royals that day. As part of the festivities, Graham baseball cards were given out to all fans in attendance, and *Field of Dreams* clips were shown on the video scoreboard between innings. The highlight came when Veda Ponikvar was invited onto the field to throw out the ceremonial first pitch.

About a year later in Dyersville, Iowa, more than 5,000 people flocked to a baseball diamond that was once a cornfield to watch the movie that had brought Doc Graham back to life. Afterward, the gathering was treated to a concert by a band featuring Kevin Costner, the film's star. It was Costner's first trip back to the mystical ball field since his work on *Field of Dreams* ended 17 years earlier.

The site, with its familiar white farmhouse and lush green grass, has hardly been forgotten, though. Owned by two local families, it has become a popular tourist attraction visited by more than 65,000 people a year. In all, more than a million pilgrims have come to the field to run the bases, reconnect with their past, and maybe even hear a voice or two out in the corn. "I think initially the natives thought interest in the field as an attraction would taper off," Dyersville mayor Jim Heavens said in 2006. "But it's been pretty steady over the years. It's one of those things that continues to make a connection with people."

The connection is just as strong in northern Minnesota, where civic leaders have decorated Lake Street with banners celebrating Chisholm as the hometown of Moonlight Graham. They have also begun construction of a state-of-the-art athletic complex named, appropriately enough, Field of Dreams, where they hope to honor their favorite son by hosting annual baseball tournaments and other youth sporting events.

In Rochester, the tributes at Doc's grave site aren't as organized, but they are usually more personal and heartfelt. Visitors to the plot—Section 9, Lot 4, IE, of Calvary Cemetery—leave candy and coins on Graham's headstone so he'll always have something in his pockets to throw to the children he loved so much. Baseballs, poetry, and other personally significant items have also been placed there. One young woman, Laura Askelin, even brought a pair of socks. They belonged to a friend who had taken them with him from Mexico to the Space Needle in Seattle and many other places in between.

Laura Askelin and her well-traveled socks have been among the many visitors to Calvary Cemetery in Rochester, Minnesota, to pay homage to Doc Graham's legacy.

Because that friend was a big fan of *Field of Dreams* in general and Graham in particular, his "Journey of the Socks" was not complete until a photo was taken at Doc's final resting place.

Who could have imagined two decades earlier that such a long-forgotten ballplayer would become so well known and so beloved? Certainly not the man who catapulted Moonlight Graham to stardom by picking his name out of the *Baseball Encyclopedia*, then writing him into a short story he was in the process of lengthening into a novel. "All I could think was, 'What a wonderful name,' " Kinsella says. "I just decided I wanted to use this guy as a character in one of my stories. My first thought was, 'What was he doing in one of the two or three coldest places in North America? He was a Southerner.' So I said to myself, 'There must be some kind of story there.' Maybe he'd been exiled or whatever. And then there was the one game and no at-bats. So I told my wife, 'Let's get up and go to Chisholm, Minnesota, and find out about him.' Of course, he turned out to be much more wonderful than anything I could have invented."

Few people are afforded a second chance at their 15 minutes of fame, especially more than a decade after they've left this earth.

But Archibald W. Graham was.

Not only that, but his second 15 minutes—this time on the silver screen—led to greater acclaim than the young ballplayer could ever have dreamed possible. Thanks to W. P. Kinsella, Moonlight Graham didn't become just a character in a book and then a hit Hollywood movie. He became a pop-culture icon.

Because of him, ballplayers who get only a brief taste of the major leagues are said to have "Moonlight Graham careers." One player's career in particular had an eerie similarity to the real thing. On July 9, 2005—only about two weeks past the 100th anniversary of Graham's big day—another young University of North Carolina graduate with the initials A. G. sprang out of a National League dugout into the bright sunlight for what proved his one and only big-league appearance. Adam Greenberg at least made it to the plate for the Chicago Cubs that day. But after being hit in the head by the first pitch he saw, or didn't see, he suffered from a form of vertigo that prevented him from returning. "If that was the extent of my time as a baseball player, just that one very strange little moment," Greenberg said during the course of an unsuccessful comeback attempt, "I guess there's nothing more I can do about it." Except, of course, to wait to be reborn on a mythical field of dreams where fact becomes fantasy and everything is possible.

So how exactly did Graham's belated fame come about? A few more details are in order.

Self-avowed baseball nut W. P. Kinsella received his copy of the *Baseball Encyclopedia* as a Christmas gift one year during the mid-1970s. While randomly flipping through the pages, the Canadian-born author stumbled across Graham's entry and decided to file it away as a potential character for a future story. The opportunity presented itself in 1978 at the Iowa Writers' Workshop, when he read aloud the title piece from his collection *Shoeless Joe Comes to Iowa.* The audience members that day enjoyed it so much that they suggested Kinsella expand it into a full-length book.

Larry Kessenich, a young editor at Houghton Mifflin, agreed and soon began assisting Kinsella in turning the short story into a novel. Though the expanded work still centered on disgraced Chicago White Sox star Shoeless Joe Jackson and a character (Ray Kinsella) who shared the same surname as his literary creator, Graham was given a major role. He became the focal point of a plot complication built around his true tale of self-sacrifice and redemption.

Among those who fell in love with the book was screen-writer and film director Phil Alden Robinson. His adaptation of W. P. Kinsella's novel not only earned an Academy Award nomination for Best Picture but opened the world's eyes to an amazing man who for too long had been overlooked. Graham "lived to be old enough that people took him for granted," says Chisholm native Bob McDonald. But thanks to Kinsella and Robinson, he has become an inspiration for those burdened with disappointment who nonetheless persevere through a lifetime of service. He represents success emerging from failure, strength built on defeat. If any two professions are respected in today's society, they are athletics and medicine. And while Graham hoped for greatness in both, he refused to allow failure in one to subdue distinction in the other.

Because of those ideals, selecting the right actor to por-tray the good doctor was important to Kinsella, Robinson, and those working with them to bring Graham back to life. Aging superstar Burt Lancaster turned in a performance that captured the spirit of a character with whom he had a lot in common. According to costar James Earl Jones, Lancaster and Graham both "had a moral point of view, a very strong one." Kinsella also thinks Lancaster was perfect for the role. "I was sorry he didn't get a [Best] Supporting Actor nomination," the author says. "He came across as such a lovable character. They tried and did a good job of making him look like Gra-ham, too." That is, except for the silvery mustache Lancaster wore for the role. Other than his distinctive bushy eyebrows, the real Graham never had any facial hair.

Graham's climactic scene is a fitting one. In it, he returns to his youth to finally get the chance to bat against a major league pitcher. After hitting a sacrifice fly and returning to the bench, he notices a young girl fall off the first-base bleach-ers and begin choking. Without thinking twice, he sprints into action and saves her. But in doing so, he realizes that he has turned back into an old man, forfeiting his opportunity to continue playing. Again, just as in reality, medicine triumphs over baseball. And as was the case nearly a century earlier, Graham isn't upset. With a twinkle in his eye, he simply picks up his black doctor's bag, says he has to get back to Alecia, and begins walking off into the sunset. Before disappearing into the corn, he turns to the other players and asks, "Win one for me, will ya, boys?"

His request is met with a reply from Shoeless Joe Jackson, played by actor Ray Liotta: "Hey, rookie, you were good."

With that, Doc glances back at the field one last time with a look Burt Lancaster biographer Kate Buford described as proclaiming, "You don't know the half of it."

In fact, even those who knew Graham best weren't fully aware of his real-life story until *Field of Dreams*. They were both thrilled and surprised when news filtered back to Chisholm that their town and its doctor were featured on film, even if they couldn't see it for themselves right away. Chisholm didn't—and still doesn't—have a movie theater. But that didn't stop erstwhile newspaper publisher Veda Ponikvar, herself a local legend played in the movie by Anne Seymour, from trying to get Universal Pictures to schedule its premiere there anyway. "I pleaded with them to have [it] in our auditorium," she said in 1989. "It's really gorgeous and it could seat 1,445 people. But they said it was their policy to go only into theaters."

To view *Field of Dreams*, people in Chisholm had to drive about 90 miles to Duluth or sit tight for a few weeks until the movie arrived in Hibbing. It turned out to be worth the wait. A few, including Doc's trusted friend Angelo Vittori, still haven't seen the movie 20 years after its release.

The film's positive effects were felt almost immediately, starting with the tourists who began trickling into town wanting to know whatever anyone could tell them about the old ballplayer turned doctor. Most were disappointed to learn that Graham's grave site wasn't in Chisholm. That, as local civic leaders realized, wasn't the only thing missing. Because nothing in town was named in their new favorite son's honor, they moved quickly to erect a banner proclaiming Chisholm the "Home of Moonlight Graham." They also renamed a new children's playground and ballpark complex "Field of Dreams." Ponikvar symbolically donated the $100 she was paid for being portrayed in the movie to help finance the $400,000 project. In recent years, the Chisholm Community Foundation has added a full-color billboard visible from Lake Street and an athletic complex to the list of Graham tributes.

But the most fitting testimonial to Doc's legacy is the impact his appearance in *Field of Dreams* has had on the community he loved so dearly. It's almost as though he's reaching out from beyond the grave to give strength to those who seek it. Michael Valentini, for instance, was so moved when he saw the movie that he decided to come back to Chisholm from Minneapolis to help manage his family's Italian restaurant. "I consider myself a dreamer," he told the *Minneapolis Star-Tribune*. So does Jim Vitali, who as a youngster was treated by Doc Graham before later serving with him as a member of the Chisholm School Board. "We have a video copy of [*Field of Dreams*] at home, and my son, grandson, and I watch it often whenever the weather precludes us from other activities," he says. "[Doc Graham] is someone I will always remember."

Vitali isn't alone. "Half the communities in North America

have a Doc Graham," W. P. Kinsella pointed out long before the specter of cynicism, greed, and performance-enhancing drugs began shrouding the game Doc loved. "We've come up here and spaded up people's memories, but what we've uncovered is all good—no paramours, no drunken binges, no opium habit, no illegitimate children, no crazy wife locked in the attic, no shady financial dealings, no evicting orphans or midnight abortions. It's a sad time when the world won't listen to stories about good men."

But now, at least, this one good man's story has been told.

What Kinsella stumbled onto in the pages of the *Baseball Encyclopedia* was a mortal who occasionally inspired the mythic, often approximated the heroic, but always remained human. Dr. Archibald W. Graham's true story is both distinctive and inspiring. Though his big-league career was only a blink of an eye, he has become a symbol for qualities Americans hold dear—dedication, selfless sacrifice, and, ultimately, the notion that with hard work and perseverance, all dreams are possible.

APPENDIX 1

Career Statistics of
Archibald Wright "Moonlight" Graham

Born: October 10, 1879, in Fayetteville, North Carolina   Position: Outfield
Died: August 25, 1965, in Chisholm, Minnesota   Height: 5–10½
Batted: Left   Weight: 175
Threw: Right   Major league debut: June 29, 1905

Year Club	League	G	AB	R	H	2B	3B	HR	SB	Avg.
1901 Tarboro	Virginia–N.C	1	3	0	0	0	0	0	0	.000
1902 Charlotte	Carolina	31	111	17	33	3	2	0	17	.297
1903 Nashua/Manchester	New England	89	342	44	82	10	7	0	30	.240
1904 Manchester	New England	108	437	70	119	15	1	0	15	.272
1905 New York	National	1	0	0	0	0	0	0	0	.000
1905 Scranton	New York State	64	264	29	76	9	3	0	10	.288
1906 Memphis	Southern Assn.	12	42	10	11	1	2	0	5	.261
1906 Scranton	New York State	124	444	65	149	15	8	1	38	.335
1907 Scranton	New York State	131	508	65	145	9	3	2	34	.265
1908 Scranton	New York State	133	506	75	140	11	5	1	32	.277

APPENDIX 2

1905 New York Giants Statistics

Manager: John McGraw
Record: 105–48
Beat the Philadelphia Athletics in the World Series, 4–1

Batting

	Pos	Age	G	AB	R	H	2B	3B	HR	RB	BB	SB	Avg.
Mike Donlin	OF	27	150	606	124	216	31	16	7	80	56	33	.356
Bob Hall	OF	26	1	3	1	1	0	0	0	0	0	0	.333
Roger Bresnahan	C	26	104	331	58	100	18	3	0	46	50	11	.302
Dan McGann	1B	33	136	491	88	147	23	14	5	75	55	22	.299
George Browne	OF	29	127	536	95	157	16	14	4	43	20	26	.293
Sam Mertes	OF	32	150	551	81	154	27	17	5	108	56	52	.279
Frank Bowerman	IF/OF	36	98	297	37	80	8	1	3	41	12	6	.269
Sammy Strang	IF	28	111	294	51	76	9	4	3	29	58	23	.259
Billy Gilbert	2B	29	115	376	45	93	11	3	0	24	41	11	.247
Art Devlin	3B	25	153	525	74	129	14	7	2	61	66	59	.246
Bill Dahlen	SS	35	148	520	67	126	20	4	7	81	62	37	.242
Boileryard Clarke	C/1B	36	31	50	2	9	0	0	1	4	4	1	.180
Offa Neal	IF	29	4	13	0	0	0	0	0	0	0	0	.000
Moonlight Graham	OF	25	1	0	0	0	0	0	0	0	0	0	.000
John McGraw	OF	32	3	0	0	0	0	0	0	0	0	1	.000

Hooks Wiltse	P	25	33	72	13	20	2	0	0	12	12	2	.278
Christy Matthewson	P	24	44	127	13	30	5	0	2	16	10	2	.236
Joe McGinnity	P	34	46	120	11	28	6	1	0	11	7	4	.233
Claude Elliott	P	28	10	16	2	3	0	0	0	0	0	0	.188
Red Ames	P	22	34	97	6	14	0	3	0	7	4	0	.144
Dummy Taylor	P	30	32	69	10	9	1	1	0	4	4	0	.130
Totals			155	5094	780	1392	191	88	39	642	517	291	.273

Pitching

	Age	G	GS	W	L	CG	SHO	IP	H	R	ER	BB	SO	ERA
C. Matthewson	24	43	37	31	9	32	8	338.6	252	85	48	64	206	1.28
Joe McGinity	34	46	38	21	15	26	2	320.3	289	131	102	71	125	2.87
Hooks Wiltse	25	32	19	15	6	18	1	197.0	158	70	54	61	120	2.47
Dummy Taylor	30	32	28	16	9	18	2	213.3	200	85	63	51	91	2.66
Red Ames	22	34	31	22	8	21	2	262.6	220	113	80	105	198	2.74
Claude Elliott	28	10	2	0	1	2	0	38.0	41	20	17	12	20	4.03
Totals		155	155	105	48	117	18	1370.0	1160	505	364	364	760	2.39

Source: baseball-reference.com

APPENDIX 3

Standings and League Leaders from Graham's Minor League Seasons

1903 New England League

	W	L	Pct.	GB	Manager
Lowell Tigers	72	41	.637	--	Fred Lake
Nashua	**68**	**46**	**.596**	**4½**	**Ed Ashenback/Chub Collins**
Manchester	**66**	**45**	**.595**	**5**	**John A. Smith**
Concord Marines	63	47	.573	7½	John Carney/Frank Eustace
Fall River Indians	57	56	.504	15	Sandy McDermott
Lawrence Colts	48	62	.436	22½	William Parsons/S. Flanagan
Brockton–New Bedford*	46	63	.422	24	Fred Doe
Haverhill Hustlers	26	86	.232	45½	Hamilton/O'Reilly/Deininger

*Moved from Brockton (18–23) to New Bedford on June 27

League Leaders

Batting: Happy Iott (Fall River)	.317
Hits: Pinky Swander (Manchester)	140
Runs: Clark Rapp (Manchester)	86
Home runs: Lou Knau (Manchester)	7
Wins: George "Lem" Cross (Lowell)	27

Pct.: George "Lem" Cross (Lowell)   .750
Strikeouts: Harry Morgan (Fall River)   197
ERA: Cy Voorhees (Manchester)   0.91

1904 New England League

	W	L	Pct	GB	Manager
Haverhill Hustlers	82	41	.667	--	Billy Hamilton
New Bedford Whalers	64	58	.525	17½	Fred Doe
Fall River Indians	65	60	.520	18	Sandy McDermott
Manchester	**61**	**60**	**.504**	**20**	**John A. Smith**
Concord Marines	62	62	.500	20½	Nathan Pulsifer
Nashua	62	62	.500	20½	John Carney/Sid Rollins
Lowell Tigers	59	62	.488	22	Fred Lake
Lawrence Colts	36	86	.295	45½	Stephen Flanagan

League Leaders
Batting: Billy Hamilton (Haverhill)   .412
Hits: Billy Hamilton (Haverhill)   168
Runs: Billy Hamilton (Haverhill)   113
Home runs: Dick Van Zant (Nashua)   7
Wins: Jim McGinley (Haverhill)   33
Pct.: Jim McGinley (Haverhill)   .825

Strikeouts: Jake Volz (Manchester)   224
ERA: Joe Yeager (Fall River)   0.98

1905 New York State League

	W	L	Pct.	GB	Manager
A.J. & G.*	71	51	.582	--	Howard Earl
Syracuse Stars	70	5	.579	½	Sandy Griffin
Wilkes-Barre Barons	70	52	.574	1	Jack Sharrott
Albany Senators	69	60	.535	5½	Connors/Doherty
Utica Pent-ups	60	60	.500	10	John Lawler
Scranton Miners	**56**	**67**	**.455**	**15½**	**Garry/Ashenback**
Binghamton Bingoes	48	75	.390	23½	Campau/Drury
Troy Trojans	51	79	.392	2	Bacon/Mason/Collins

*Amsterdam-Johnstown-Gloversville

League Leaders
Batting: John Seigle (Wilkes-Barre)   .344
Runs: Rube DeGroff (Troy)   85
Hits: John Seigle (Wilkes-Barre)   159
Wins: George Bell (A.J. & G.)   25
Pct.: George Bell (A.J. & G.)   .676

1906 New York State League

	W	L	Pct.	GB	Manager
Scranton Miners	**82**	**48**	**.631**	--	**Ed Ashenback**
Albany Senators	73	63	.537	12	Michael Doherty
Syracuse Stars	70	65	.519	14½	Sandy Griffin
Troy Trojans	67	64	.511	15½	John O'Brien
A.J. & G. Jags	66	68	.493	17½	Howard Earl
Utica Pent-ups	61	72	.459	22	John Lawler
Binghamton Bingoes	58	72	.446	23½	Robert Drury
Wilkes-Barre Barons	52	76	.406	29	Sharrott/Donovan

League Leaders
Batting: **Moonlight Graham (Scranton)** **.335***
Runs: Leo Hafford (A.J. & G.) 86
Hits: Rube DeGroff (Troy) 160
Wins: Billy Chappelle (Albany) 27
Pct.: Billy Chappelle (Albany) .794

*In some sources, Graham's average is rounded up to .336 to break the tie with Weaver of A.J. & G. Graham went 149 for 444 (.335585), while Weaver went 159 for 474 (.335443).

1907 New York State League

	W	L	Pct.	GB	Manager
Albany Senators	79	50	.612	--	Michael Doherty
Scranton Miners	**81**	**54**	**.600**	**1**	**Henry Ramsey**
Utica Pent-ups	78	54	.591	2½	Charles Dooley
Troy Trojans	75	56	.573	5	John O'Brien
Wilkes-Barre Barons	69	66	.511	13	Abel Lizotte
Syracuse Stars	61	75	.449	21½	Sandy Griffin
Binghamton Bingoes	51	83	.381	30½	Robert Drury
A.J. & G. Jags	31	95	.291	42½	Howard Earl

League Leaders
Batting: Wally Hollingsworth (Wilkes-Barre)   .327
Runs: Fred Eley (Wilkes-Barre)   76
Hits: Rube DeGroff (Troy)   151
Wins: Bill Schlitzer (Utica)   27
Pct.: Bill Schlitzer (Utica)   .711
Strikeouts: Bill Schlitzer (Utica)   207

1908 New York State League

	W	L	Pct.	GB	Manager
Scranton Miners	**84**	**51**	**.622**	--	**Mal Kittredge**
Binghamton Bingoes	80	61	.567	7	Jimmy Bannon
Troy Trojans	78	61	.561	9	John O'Brien
Syracuse Stars	76	64	.543	10½	Sandy Griffin
Utica Pent-ups	74	64	.536	11½	Charles Dooley
Albany Senators	67	73	.479	19½	Michael Doherty
Wilkes-Barre Barons	60	77	.438	25	Lizotte/Drury
A.J. & G./Elmira Colonels*	36	104	.257	50½	Bacon/Ramsey

*Amsterdam-Johnstown-Gloversville (11–54) moved to Elmira on July 22.

League Leaders
Batting: Gene Goode (Troy)   .304
Runs: Jim Tamsett (Albany)   88
Hits: Gene Goode (Troy)   153
Stolen bases: Art Marcan (Troy)   65

Source: www.baseball-reference.com

APPENDIX 4

Field of Dreams
Film vs. Fact

Film	Fact
Moonlight Graham played one inning in right field against the Dodgers.	Graham actually played two innings in right and was on deck when the game ended.
The Fenway Park scoreboard says Graham played his one major league game in 1922.	Graham played in his one major league game on June 29, 1905.
Graham tells Ray Kinsella that his one game came on the final day of the season.	Graham stayed with the Giants a few more days before being sent to the minors, where he played the rest of the season in Scranton, Pennsylvania.
Graham tells Kinsella that he retired to become a doctor, rather than being sent back to the minors.	Graham played three more full seasons, getting his medical certification and setting up his first practice while still playing in Scranton.

Graham takes Kinsella to his office in downtown Chisholm.	Because Graham worked for the school system, his office was in the Washington School about three blocks east of downtown.
Kinsella meets Graham in 1972.	Graham died in 1965.
Graham tells Kinsella that he was born in Chisholm.	Graham was born in Fayetteville, North Carolina.
Graham tells Kinsella that his father was a doctor.	Alexander Graham was a noted educator who held a law degree from Columbia University.
Burt Lancaster wore a mustache while portraying the elderly Graham.	The real Graham never had facial hair.
Young Archie Graham bats right handed.	Graham was a left-handed hitter.
Graham wears a uniform with the name *Giants* in red across the chest.	The Giants' uniforms in 1905 had the block letters *N* and *Y* in blue across the chest.

The action takes place in Chisholm, Minnesota.

The Chisholm scenes were actually filmed in Galena, Illinois.

Acknowledgments

Senator Hillary Clinton once wrote that it takes a village to raise a child. That may or may not be the case. But this much is certain—the true story of *Field of Dreams* doctor Archibald W. "Moonlight" Graham could not have been told without the help, love, and support of an entire town.

Chisholm, Minnesota, is not unlike most other small Rust Belt cities across the upper Midwest. It has a quaint main street, a dwindling population, and a proud sense of community and tradition. It is so typical that when the producers began filming *Field of Dreams,* they chose another small locale in the Midwest—Galena, Illinois—to stand in for Chisholm. Those producers, however, failed to recognize the one thing that sets Chisholm apart from most other places like it—the people who live there. This book would still be a dream if not for their support, their hospitality, and, of course, their wonderful stories of the man they knew simply as "Doc."

We especially appreciate the efforts and knowledge of Veda Ponikvar, an amazing woman whose energy, leadership, and zest for public service remain as strong today in her 80s as they were when she was a crusading young newspaper publisher and political activist in the 1960s. Her life would also make a good biography. With all due respect to Anne Seymour, who played Veda in the movie, no one could possibly duplicate the real thing. Veda also bakes darn good cookies and other pastries, especially around Christmastime.

Another indispensable member of the Chisholm community is Ron Gornik. A retired banker and tireless local activist, he served as chairman of the Chisholm Community Foundation during the time we were researching this book. Not only did Ron open up his house, loan his car, and make other sacrifices to help bring Doc Graham's story to the public, he also used his considerable clout to arrange the financing of several trips from North Carolina to Minnesota. We owe him a debt we can never repay in full, either financially or spiritually.

We would also like to thank Mike Kalibabky, the dedicated founder of the Doc Graham Scholarship Fund, and his wife, Mary Ann, who happily served as tour guides and hosts while sharing their vast collection of Moonlight knowledge and their recipe for almond bark candy; Angelo Vittori, the youngest 90-year-old in history; Mary Giannini, for taking us into her house and telling us stories; Pat Blacker of Northwest Airlines and Richard Newbauer of the Chisholm Inn & Suites, for helping with air travel and accommodations; head librarian Steve Harsin and his staff at the Iron Range Research Center; and the other Chisholmites who played major roles in making this project a reality, including Bob McDonald, Frank Tancabel, Mary Vecchi Russo, the late Jerry Samsa, Jim Vitali, Florene Luther, the Taconite Chapter of the Free and Accepted Masons, the owners of Valentini's Supper Club, Frances Russ, Marie Tolanen, and city assessor Steve Erickson. We also thank Joanne Dornack Brownell of Hibbing.

In Rochester, we were fortunate enough to meet up with Lynn Williamson Didier, Alecia Graham's great-niece and the unofficial historian for the entire Madden family. Her contribution to this book would have been invaluable had she only driven us to the Grahams' grave site, the old Madden farm where Alecia and Docky's wedding was held, and the Mayo Estate. But she also fed us the best homemade wild rice soup in Minnesota and introduced us to her uncle Bob Madden and his beautiful wife, Nan, who had their own interesting memories and stories to tell. Most of all, though, Lynn generously shared her years of research, along with pictures and other artifacts, allowing us a look inside the intimate relationship of a remarkable couple.

In Scranton, Pennsylvania, the town where Graham played four minor league seasons and nearly stayed for good, we were aided by Ed Christine, sports editor of the *Scranton Times-Tribune*, and Brian Fulton, the newspaper's library manager; Cheryl Kshuba, Mary Ann Moran, and Marian Yevics of the Lackawanna Historical Society; and the management of the minor league team known at the time as the Scranton–Wilkes-Barre Red Barons.

Closer to home (and Moonlight's birthplace), we benefited from the support of the administration at the University of North Carolina–Pembroke and the editors and staff of the *Fayetteville Observer*. This book began as a story in the *Observer*'s sports section. It would never have grown beyond that if not for the newspaper's Pat Reese Fellowship and the generosity and faith of publisher Charles Broadwell. No one has greater love for Fayetteville and the newspaper that serves it. Other important contributors at the paper included former sports editor Doug Kennedy; sportswriters Thomas Pope, Sammy Batten, Earl Vaughn, Dan Wiederer, and Mike Graff; local historian Roy Parker, Jr.; and librarian *extraordinaire* Daisy Maxwell.

Daisy was one of many helpful librarians we leaned upon heavily while "chasing Moonlight." Those divas of the Dewey

Decimal System included Sarah Klemmer of the *Charlotte Observer*, Betsey Moylan of the University of Scranton, Evelyn Gibbons of the Lackawanna County (Pennsylvania) Library System, Deb Fuehrer of the Mayo Clinic's Eisenberg Library, and the research staff of the University of North Carolina's Wilson Library.

Though we never actually got to meet them in person, we would also like to thank interns Liam Bowen and Elizabeth Terry of the Baseball Hall of Fame in Cooperstown, New York, and Richard Bheles and Karen Buckelew of the University of Maryland for their research assistance. The same is true for former New York Giants general manager and *Charlotte News* reporter Ernie Accorsi; former major leaguer, American League president, and cardiologist Dr. Bobby Brown; and the staff of the Society for American Baseball Research.

Despite all this assistance, *Chasing Moonlight* would still be nothing more than the dream of a sportswriter and a college professor if not for the faith and vision of Carolyn Sakowski, president of John F. Blair, Publisher, and editor Steve Kirk. Carolyn saw something many others overlooked in the manuscript and the man whose story it tells. For that, we will be forever grateful. We are even more appreciative of Steve's contribution to this project. His criticism wasn't always what we wanted to hear, but it was honest, direct, and, as is usually the case with talented editors, right on the money. He was always available when we needed him. His unwavering passion for Moonlight Graham's story helped keep us going even when it seemed we would never get it to print.

Finally, we would like to extend our sincere gratitude and admiration to the great W. P. Kinsella, without whom our chase would never have been necessary. Having an opportunity to talk to and exchange stories with such a distinguished author was one of the highlights of the two and a half years it took to complete this book.

And lest we forget, thank you to our families for their love, support, and encouragement, without which you would not be reading these words today. We love you all!

6/10